Informal Care of the Elderly

Informal Care
of the Elderly

Susan A. Stephens
Mathematica Policy Research, Inc.

Jon B. Christianson
University of Arizona

Lexington Books
D.C. Heath and Company / Lexington, Massachusetts / Toronto

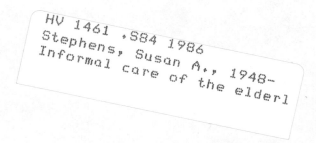
Library of Congress Cataloging-in-Publication Data

Stephens, Susan A., 1948–
  Informal care of the elderly.

  Bibliography: p.
  Includes index.
  1. Aged—Home care—United
States. 2. Aged—United States—Family relationships. I. Christianson, Jon B.
II. Title.
HV1461.S84 1985   362.6'3   85–45159
ISBN 0–669–11227–5 (alk. paper)

Published simultaneously in Canada
Printed in the United States of America
Casebound International Standard Book Number: 0–669–11227–5
Library of Congress Catalog Card Number: 85–45159

The paper used in this publication meets the minimum requirements of American
National Standard for Information Sciences—Permanence of Paper for Printed Library
Materials, ANSI Z39.48–1984.

The last numbers on the right below indicate the number and date of printing.

10 9 8 7 6 5 4 3 2 1

95 94 93 92 91 90 89 88 87 86

Contents

Tables

Preface

T he purpose of this book is to describe in detail the characteristics and experiences of individuals who regularly provide assistance to their frail elderly relatives and friends. National policy efforts have increasingly focused on strategies for reducing the public costs of institutionalization; as a result, interest in informally provided services—the major source of care for most elderly Americans—has also heightened. It is the efforts of these informal caregivers that enable many elderly people to remain living in the community, outside of nursing homes and other long-term care institutions. This book adds to the growing body of research on informal care to the elderly by providing a detailed picture of the everyday effort of nearly two thousand individuals, each of whom was identified as the primary caregiver to an elderly person at risk of institutionalization.

This book is based on data collected for an evaluation of the National Long-Term Care Demonstration (more commonly known as the "channeling demonstration"), which was conducted by Mathematica Policy Research (MPR), Inc., and its subcontractors for the U.S. Department of Health and Human Services, under contract number HHS–100–80–0157. The findings discussed herein were first presented in a technical report to the government.

The technical report and this book represent the result of the contributions of many people working on the evaluation of the channeling demonstration. The baseline caregiver survey instrument was developed by Barbara Phillips and Diana Davis, with expert advice from Marjorie Cantor of Fordham University's Center on Gerontology, Barbara Schneider of Temple University's Institute of Aging, and Phyllis Thorburn, now with the National Center for Health Statistics. Many staff members participated in the data collection and coding process, and were ably supervised and assisted by Joanna Cerf, Todd Ensor, Audrey McDonald, Patricia Rossi, Nadine Rubenstein, Carol Wolff, and Belva Wood.

Important contributions to the quantitative sections of the book were made by MPR programmers Dan Buckley, Nancy Holden, and Ira Trachtenberg. Helpful comments and suggestions on the many drafts of the technical report were provided by Robert Applebaum, Randall Brown, George Carcagno, Peter Kemper, Barbara Phillips, and Craig Thornton (all from Mathematica Policy Research); by Raymond Baxter, now at New York City Health and Hospitals Corporation; and by Robert Clark and Carolyn Miller of the Department of Health and Human Services. Editorial assistance in the preparation of the technical report was provided by Felicity Skidmore; many people helped produce the report: Johanna Baker, Anne Ciemnecki, Vicki Dixon, Denise Dunn, Donna Fersch, Sheila Howlett, Marian Johnson, Rose Pannell, Joann Peate, Celeste Rye, Judy Wayno, and Jennifer Webb.

We especially wish to thank Mathematica Policy Research for supporting the efforts to revise the technical report and to produce this book. Anna Baan and Rhoda Cohen carried out the tedious tasks of tracking down citations and preparing the bibliography, and Celeste Rye, Denise Dunn, and Tracy Ream prepared the manuscript. In particular, Thomas Good provided valuable editorial support; without his guidance, the process of making revisions to the organization, style, and format of the original manuscript would have been considerably more tedious and, to the degree that we can claim any success in transforming a technical report to a more broadly accessible book, less successful.

Finally, we wish to thank the caregivers who provided the information summarized in this report. They generously gave the time necessary for the interview, which often had to be scheduled not simply around outside employment and other family responsibilities, but, more importantly, around their caregiving responsibilities to their elderly relatives, friends, or neighbors.

1
Public Policy and Informal Support for the Elderly

For the past several decades, the median age of the U.S. population has been rising, and the elderly segment of the population has been living longer. These two demographic trends have heightened concern about the rising costs of providing long-term care in nursing homes and other institutions and about the drain on both public and private resources induced by these rising expenditures. A major thrust of public policy in this area has focused on ways to minimize the use of nursing homes and other long-term care facilities and to rely increasingly on less expensive home-care services to help elderly persons remain in the community if feasible. A vital resource for community-based care is the informal support network of family, friends, neighbors, and community volunteers—that is, informal caregivers. This network, which is already an important component of such care, has also become a much-discussed option by policymakers and care planners.

Various policy initiatives and programmatic approaches have been proposed to maintain and, if possible, increase the level of informally provided services. These efforts have been based on available knowledge about informal caregiving and caregivers and on assumptions about how informal support is likely to respond to changes in the incentives and services provided by the formal care system. For example, as we will discuss in greater detail in this chapter, policy strategies to sustain informal caregiving by providing financial payments to family members have been based on the assumption that such incentives address an overriding concern of many potential caregivers—that financial considerations are an important factor in their decisions about whether to provide informal care. Appropriate choices among policy approaches depend at least partially on the validity and generalizability of such assumptions and, consequently, on the current body of knowledge on informal caregiving.

This book attempts to fill some of the existing gaps in our knowledge of informal caregiving by examining the experiences of a large and diverse group of caregivers, all of whom provide substantial care to frail elderly persons who need such assistance in order to remain in the community. Our purpose is to provide a detailed and broad-range picture of how informal care is currently provided to the frail elderly, in the belief that a more in-depth understanding both of the nature of informal caregiving and of the characteristics and experiences of informal caregivers will enable decisionmakers to develop more informed policy in this important health service area. We do not intend to recommend one policy approach over another; rather, our effort will be descriptive in nature, setting the findings of this study within the context of previous research, as we highlight each of several aspects of caregiving throughout the book.

Before presenting our findings in subsequent chapters, we first review the role of informal caregivers in the current system of long-term care for the elderly, summarize the alternative policy approaches for providing informal care, and identify the limitations of the existing body of knowledge. The remainder of our introductory chapter addresses each of these topics in turn.

The Role of Informal Caregivers

Substantial evidence suggests that informal caregivers are the primary providers of sustained care to the elderly. For example, over a decade ago, a national survey of persons ages 55 and over who were receiving care at home indicated that in four of every five cases at least some portion of the care was provided by a relative (National Center for Health Statistics 1972, 8). In a more recent survey of the elderly in New York City, families provided 77 percent of the services that were judged to be most important in delaying institutionalization (Gurland et al. 1978, 21–22). In Cleveland, Ohio, this figure was found to be as high as 80 percent of the severely impaired elderly (General Accounting Office 1977, 20).

Family members and other informal supports are very often the elderly person's preferred source of care (see Cicirelli 1981). When asked on whom they would rely in an emergency or for assistance with personal care, medications, or transportation, 45 percent of the elderly persons in a study in New York City named a child or other relative (Cantor 1977). Substantially fewer (25 percent) named a friend or neighbor, but still fewer requested assistance through formal services. Family members (particularly adult children) are generally willing to take on caregiving responsibilities (see Brody 1981), and most elderly apparently feel that their families are doing all they can to provide the care they need (see Lewis et al. 1980).

Both the elderly and their families strongly resist nursing-home placement, and families contribute a great deal toward preventing or delaying this move (see Shanas 1979 and Schorr 1980). Thus, informal care can be an effective strategy for helping some impaired elderly remain in the community. For example, a study by Anderson, Patten, and Greenberg (1980) comparing home care with nursing-home care among elderly persons in Minnesota found that the group receiving help at home from two or more informal sources was more impaired on average than a group of elderly residents of nursing homes classified as intermediate-care facilities.

These informal caregiving efforts, while largely successful in helping the elderly avoid institutionalization, very often place heavy demands on the caregivers, taking a toll on their emotional and often physical well-being (see Cantor 1983; Cicirelli 1981; and Caro and Blank 1984).[1] Informal caregivers are typically involved in personal care and such other daily household tasks as meal preparation; many provide care, socialization, and/or supervision on a round-the-clock basis. In addition to providing assistance to the elderly person, many caregivers must juggle a number of conflicting demands on their time and energies—for instance, providing sufficient attention to (other) family members (spouse and/or children) and to job demands. Caregiving also means that caregivers must often sacrifice their own desires for leisure and freedom in pursuing their own interests—which is particularly stressful for adult children who may have just completed child-rearing responsibilities, or for adults who themselves have just reached retirement. Given the demands of caregiving itself and the stress associated with meeting what are very often the continually increasing needs of the elderly care recipient, it is hardly surprising that caregivers often request services which provide respite care—help with daily household tasks—to enable them to take occasional time away from their caregiving responsibilities.

Policy Issues in Informal Care

There is no question that defining the appropriate role for family members and other informal caregivers in the evolving long-term care system has become a matter of increasing concern for policymakers at both the state and federal levels (see, for example, Callahan et al. 1980; Health Care Financing Administration 1981; Taber, Anderson, and Rogers 1980; Demkovich 1979; and Congressional Budget Office 1977). As is true with many policy concerns in the 1980s, the motivation for the current study on informal caregivers is primarily economic. Expenditures for long-term care services of all types have been increasing at a rapid rate, as has the public sector's share of these expenditures (Clark and Menefee 1981). The public cost of nursing-home care alone was $12 billion in 1980 and is projected to reach $43 billion by 1990 (Somers 1982, 222). Because of the sustained and projected growth in the population which is most vulnerable to the chronic mental and physical conditions that require long-term care—the elderly over 75 years of age—increases in public expenditures are expected to continue and even to accelerate. This view of the future has spurred policymakers to search for alternative, less expensive approaches for financing and delivering long-term care. Since informal caregivers provide most of the long-term care in this country, the impact of system reforms on them has important implications in terms of the cost-effectiveness of these efforts and their ultimate acceptability as policy interventions. In this section, we describe three types of interventions currently being advocated in the design and support of community-based care for the elderly, and we link the assumptions behind these interventions to what is known about the dynamics of informal care.

The Substitution of Community-Based Care for Institutional Care

The government-funded demonstration from which the data for this book were derived (see chapter 2) is representative of one approach for reforming the system of delivering long-term care services. It builds on the past experience of a variety of smaller experimental programs implemented at the state and local levels (see Greenberg et al. 1980). The common feature of all of these efforts is an attempt to substitute community-based services (for example, home health care, housekeeping and home services, transportation, and the delivery of prepared meals) for presumably more expensive institutional services. The extent to which these reform efforts are ultimately adopted on a wider scale by the public sector seems likely to depend on two factors: whether community services can be directed toward those persons who would use institutional care otherwise, so as actually to reduce the use of publicly reimbursed hospitals and nursing homes, and whether the availability of community services leads to their substitution for care that was previously provided by family or friends. If substitution occurs to a significant degree, then public programs that subsidize community-based care are likely to be politically unacceptable; they will be viewed as a waste of tax dollars devoted to purchasing services that would have been provided at no expense to the public purse.

Although the potential importance of the substitution issue is clearly significant in terms of designing public-sector strategies to reform long-term care, its empirical relevance remains largely unexplored. In particular, little is known about how families and other sources of informal care would be likely to respond if publicly funded in-home services for the elderly were more widely available. The utility of studies that have been undertaken on this issue has been limited by their small, narrowly drawn samples and, in some cases, by their methodological shortcomings. The measures that have been used provide only partial insight into whether or not substitution exists. For example, Lewis et al. (1980, 6–7) observed both decreases and increases in the percentage of specific types of services provided by caregivers. Greene (1983) and Talbott, Smith, and Miller (1982) have found that the number of different areas in which informal care was provided became less as the number of areas in which formal services were provided became greater. However, this scenario may reflect specialization on the part of informal caregivers rather than an overall reduction in their level of effort.

The data presented in this book suggest that the substitution issue must be explored by researchers on a broader basis if it is to be addressed convincingly. As we will discuss in chapter 4, primary caregivers typically provide a variety of services as part of their caregiving activities. Given this variety in caregiving activities, the provision of formal care may well reduce caregiving in one area and increase it in another. Second, based on the findings presented in this book, it seems unlikely that primary caregivers will withdraw entirely from caregiving activities when subsidized community-based care becomes available, given both the intimacy of their relationship and their intense involvement with the care recipient. Clearly, measures that are sensitive to the degree of involvement must be used to assess the substitution issue. Third, in addressing the substitution issue, researchers must focus on the financial contributions of caregivers. As we will show in chapter 6, a large proportion of caregivers in this study also provided financial assistance, and a reduction in caregiving activities could be accompanied by increases in financial assistance. Finally, the data presented throughout this book confirm the hypothesis that caregiving activities vary according to the caregiver's living situation and to his or her relationship to the care recipient. Thus, the variations in the possible effects of substitution for these and other characteristics of caregivers must be examined thoroughly, since it may be possible to minimize the substitution for specific types of caregivers and caregiving relationships.

Reimbursement of Caregivers

The provision of financial support to informal caregivers is an alternative to direct government support for formal, community-based long-term care for the elderly. This approach to reducing the institutionalization of the impaired elderly first received national attention in 1975, with the introduction of Senate Bill 1161 (see Prager 1978). The intent of this particular piece of proposed legislation was to increase the level of in-home care provided by low-income families to impaired elderly relatives through the use of financial incentives.

While Senate Bill 1161 was not passed, several states have developed various programs to provide financial assistance to caregivers. California pioneered this effort, but apparently experienced considerable difficulty in administering the program. Other states, including Texas, Oklahoma, Wisconsin, and New York, have implemented more limited efforts (see Callahan et al. 1980). Recently, Arling and McAuley (1983) reviewed the feasibility of public financing to encourage the continued involvement of informal caregivers, based on their analysis of an ongoing family support program in the state of Virginia. They point out that the success of financial assistance to families in increasing their informal care to elderly relatives depends, for example, on the willingness of families to take on such responsibilities and on the importance of financial considerations in the decision to provide care. As documented both in this book (see especially chapters 3 and 4) and in many other studies, family members and other informal sources of care are clearly capable of and willing to provide a relatively large amount of care. However, the evidence on financial considerations is much more questionable. The data presented in chapters 6 and 7 suggest that the financial burden of caregiving is likely to be of little concern to many caregivers; other aspects of the burden, particularly emotional strain, are much more important. However, our findings on the well-being of caregivers do suggest that the financial strain experienced by caregivers is associated with their own income levels. Should they be adopted, programs to provide financial support to caregivers could well achieve their greatest success if they were targeted toward lower-income caregivers.

Obviously, many considerations must be weighed when programs are developed to provide financial support to informal caregivers. For example, how will payments be monitored and fraud and abuse discouraged? Would even the most generous program help elderly persons who live alone? What form would the support take? How would it change the values and motivations of caregivers? And would payments reduce the "caring" aspect of the caregiving relationship? Although the data presented in this book cannot address these issues, they do call into question the fundamental premises that financial burden is a key limiting factor in the degree to which caregivers can provide care, and that it contributes to the premature institutionalization of the care recipient.

Social Support for Caregivers

Community service agencies are increasingly involved in providing support services to their elderly clients' families and other informal caregiv-

ers.[2] In particular, they have been devoting their efforts to developing
strategies for strengthening the capacity of informal supports to continue, and perhaps even expand, their caregiving activities. Such support
services can include, for example, the provision of equipment or training
to assist in physically strenuous or medical tasks. Moreover, lessening
the stress experienced by caregivers—by providing education on the process of aging and the specific diseases or disabilities of the elderly, by
offering access to support groups or counseling, or by providing respite
services—is also judged to have an impact on institutionalization decisions by mitigating or obviating the "burn out" phenomenon. Supporting the informal care network through these activities can be effective in
terms of strengthening the family unit with minimal intervention and
reducing public costs for both community-based and institutional care.

The success of such efforts depends in part on the appropriateness
of several underlying assumptions about the concept and nature of informal care. As we mentioned, one such assumption seems well sup-
ported—that psychological stress is more likely to be a critical factor in
the breakdown of informal caregiving than are financial or physical burdens. Much of the support offered by community agencies is designed to
help caregivers deal with emotional stress through counseling, education,
support groups, and respite care. Less is known about other assumptions
surrounding such an approach. For example, can the provision of social
supports create an informal system that did not exist previously and
motivate others to become secondary sources of informal care in an
effort to help the primary caregiver, or are social supports effective only
with an already functioning network? How effective is such support as
the elderly person's condition deteriorates or as the caregiver's own circumstances change? At what point must formal services, in addition to
social support, be provided to avoid a breakdown in informal caregiving
and to avoid institutionalization? Definitive answers to these questions
require data on the impact of support services over a period of time with
a variety of caregivers. While this study cannot address the effectiveness
of social support to caregivers directly, it does provide detailed information on the threshold level at which informal caregivers reported the
need for assistance in the form of formal services. This threshold is high
(see chapter 5), and, in the eyes of both family members and profession-
als, elderly persons who require a large amount of informal services are
still capable of remaining in the community *if* the informal system is
supplemented with formal in-home services. Obviously, thresholds at
which formal intervention is requested or required vary for different
caregivers and caregiving situations, but, in many cases, it appears that
social support to the caregivers is not sufficient in itself to maintain the
level of informal care necessary to enable the frail elderly person to remain in the community.

Research Issues in Informal Care

As the first step in designing strategies to reform the system, one must acquire as accurate and as detailed a picture of the existing system as possible. Information is available to describe the formal service components of that system, such as nursing homes and home health agencies; in particular, the Medicare and Medicaid programs routinely collect information on these providers as part of their reimbursement procedures, and, in some cases, state licensing agencies and provider associations also collect the data necessary to inform policymakers. However, the basic information available on informal caregivers is much more limited, even though these caregivers are, and are likely to continue to be, the most important component of the overall long-term care system.

This situation is changing rapidly. A number of studies have been completed in recent years that address various aspects of the caregiving experience, such as the relationship between caregivers and the elderly care recipients, the presence of reciprocal caregiving, the types of services provided by informal caregivers, the amount of time and money devoted to caregiving activities, the burden perceived by caregivers, and the impact of caregiving on the economic and emotional well-being of caregivers.

As extensive as the literature on informal caregiving is becoming, it continues to suffer from a number of limitations in terms of providing an adequate base of knowledge. Most studies have been small in scale, including samples of only a few hundred or even a much smaller number of caregivers. Most have also been local in scope, focusing on the elderly only in a single city or in another geographically limited area. Some have provided data on the elderly person or the caregiver but not both, and many have focused on a relatively narrow spectrum of potential issues of interest. Studies to date have also varied in terms of the impairment or need levels of the elderly included in the research, and in terms of how informal caregivers are defined. Consequently, while the most basic findings from these studies have been consistent—that is, that most elderly who need assistance receive informal care, that caregivers are most often family members and particularly women (wives, daughters, and daughters-in-law), that most caregiving involves personal care and household tasks rather than medical care, and that caregiving imposes stress on caregivers—the details of the caregiving experience have not been described with any degree of confidence.

Gaps in the current body of knowledge on informal caregiving are particularly acute in terms of the frequency with which various caregiving activities are performed, the amount of time devoted to them, and the prevalence and amount of financial assistance provided by informal caregivers. In addition, measuring the consequences of caregiving is a complex issue, and a variety of definitions and approaches, both objective and subjective, have been adopted. What has been missing is a single dataset which links caregiving with a number of variables that characterize the well-being of caregivers, rather than with only one or two of such variables.

We believe that the information provided in this book is unique and can be particularly useful to policymakers in several respects. First, it focuses on the caregiving provided to *highly impaired* elderly, the likely target group for system reform. Thus, it provides information on those caregiving networks that are of the greatest current interest to public policymakers. Second, the data are drawn from multiple sites, and the sample size is large relative to other studies. Both of these considerations enhance the utility of the descriptive findings for developing policy. Finally, data were collected along a broad array of caregiving dimensions, providing a relatively complete picture of the informal care system and the well-being of caregivers.

Chapter 2 describes in detail the study from which the data for this book were drawn. Subsequent chapters address various substantive issues that pertain to informal caregiving, including the characteristics of primary caregivers (chapter 3), the type and amount of care they provide (chapter 4), the broader informal care network (chapter 5), the financial contributions associated with informal caregiving (chapter 6), and measures of the well-being of caregivers (chapter 7).

Notes

1. We should say that several studies have also noted that, while most caregivers show some emotional and other effects from the demands of caregiving, not all caregivers are affected to a degree that harms their own physical health or emotional well-being (see Fengler and Goodrich 1979; Poulshock 1982; Zarit, Reever, and Bach-Peterson 1980). Moreover, as Brody (1985) notes in her summary of long-term care to elderly parents, such efforts have become normative—they are not uncommon, and some tacit rules do apply to them.

2. For example, under the direction of staff at the Temple University Institute on Aging (the technical assistance contractor for the demonstration), a monograph is being prepared to document the efforts to support informal caregiving networks that are being undertaken by the projects involved in the National Long-Term Care Demonstration.

2
The Channeling Study of Informal Caregivers

I n September 1980, the U.S. Department of Health and Human Services initiated a national experiment that has come to be known as the "channeling demonstration." The purpose of the demonstration was to test whether a carefully managed approach for providing community-based long-term care would help control the costs of care while maintaining or improving the well-being of its elderly clients. As part of the overall evaluation of the demonstration, one research component focused on informal caregivers and the impacts that channeling services might have on the informal caregiving experience.

The Channeling Intervention

The National Long-Term Care Demonstration, or channeling demonstration, was designed to serve elderly persons (persons who were sixty-five years of age or older) residing in the catchment areas of the ten demonstration projects who were presumed to be at risk of institutionalization, but who, with assistance, were expected to be able to live in the community.[1] "At risk of institutionalization" was operationalized as meeting criteria on both functional disability and unmet needs. Under the functional disability criterion, an elderly person must have exhibited one of the following conditions: two moderate disabilities in performing activities of daily living (ADL),[2] three severe impairments in his or her ability to perform instrumental activities of daily living (IADL),[3] or one severe ADL disability and two severe IADL impairments. Cognitive or behavioral difficulties that affected an individual's ability to perform activities of daily living could count as one of the severe IADL impairments. The second criterion (the existence of unmet needs) was fulfilled if needs for two or more services were not expected to be met for a period of at least six months. A fragile informal support system which was not expected to be able to continue to meet the needs of the client also provided evidence of unmet needs.

The channeling intervention consisted of seven components:[4]

1. *Outreach* to identify and attract potential clients at high risk of entering a long-term care institution

2. *Standardized eligibility screening* to determine whether an applicant met preestablished criteria

3. *Comprehensive in-person assessment* to identify the problems, resources, and service needs of individual clients, in preparation for developing a care plan

4. *Initial care planning* to specify the types and amount of care required to meet the identified needs of clients

5. *Service arrangement* to implement the care plan through the provision of both formal and informal in-home and community services

6. *Ongoing monitoring* to ensure that services were appropriately delivered and continued to meet the needs of clients

7. *Periodic reassessment* to adjust care plans to the changing needs of clients

The entire channeling demonstration consisted of ten participating states and local agencies, a technical assistance contractor, and a national evaluation contractor. The channeling projects were located in Baltimore, Maryland; Houston, Texas; Middlesex County, New Jersey; eastern Kentucky; York and Cumberland counties in Southern Maine; Miami, Florida; Greater Lynn, Massachusetts; Rensselaer County, New York; Cuyahoga County (including Cleveland), Ohio; and Philadelphia, Pennsylvania. The projects began accepting clients from February to June of 1982, and were fully operational through October 1984. The local projects were phased out of the federal program in March 1985, although most continued to operate under other auspices.

Evaluation of the Channeling Demonstration

The evaluation was based on an experimental design in which the outcomes of channeling were compared with what would have occurred in the absence of the demonstration services.[5] Persons who were referred to each channeling project (typically by a service provider or a family member) were interviewed, usually by telephone, to determine whether they met the channeling eligibility criteria. If eligible, they were assigned randomly to either a treatment group (which had the opportunity to participate in channeling) or a control group (which continued to rely on the services that were otherwise available in the community). Both groups received a standardized assessment after consenting to participate in the research.[6]

In addition to the surveys of elderly channeling participants, another survey was administered to the individuals who were identified by the elderly as their primary informal caregivers. Given budget and schedule constraints, it was not feasible to use the entire group of elderly demonstration participants as the basis for the caregiver survey. Instead, the caregiver study was based on those persons who were providing assistance to the elderly persons who entered the demonstration between November 15, 1982, and May 27, 1982.[7]

This book is based primarily on the data from the first interview conducted with those persons who were identified as the primary informal caregivers to the elderly demonstration participants, although some information on the elderly themselves is also included. The survey that was administered to primary informal caregivers is described in the following section.

Survey of Primary Informal Caregivers

The primary informal caregiver was defined as the friend or family member who provided the greatest amount of assistance to the elderly care recipient in terms of taking care of him or her, attending to his or her affairs, or performing chores around the house. When the elderly study participants were interviewed, they were asked to name this caregiver and to give written permission for a research interviewer to contact the person. Screening information was collected from the designated caregivers to determine whether they met the study definition of primary informal caregiver.

Friends or family members who helped with one or more of the following tasks were considered to meet the study definition:

1. Medical care:
   Physical, occupational, or speech therapy
   Other medical treatments
2. Personal care:
   Eating
   Getting out of bed or a chair
   Dressing
   Bathing
   Getting to or using the toilet
   Cleaning up after bladder or bowel accidents
3. Giving medicines or injections

4. Meal preparation

5. Housework, laundry, or shopping

6. Chores (heavy housework and minor repairs)

7. Transportation and escort

8. Managing financial affairs

9. Supervision for personal safety (staying with the elderly person because he or she could not be left alone)

10. Arranging for benefits or services and dealing with providers

11. Minor errands

If more than one friend or family member helped with these tasks, the one who provided the greatest amount of assistance in the judgment of the care recipient was designated as the primary informal caregiver. Friends or family members whose *only* form of assistance to the sample member was emotional or financial support were excluded from the survey. Family members who were paid for their assistance were included if they met the other criteria. Employees and volunteers from service organizations were included only if they reported that they had been friends of the care recipient prior to their providing care.

In addition to the types of care provided and the relationship between the caregiver and the care recipient, a third element of the definition focused on the frequency with which help was provided. Caregivers were either to be providing assistance on a regular basis (at least once a month) at the time of their interview or to have been providing assistance on a regular basis either in the month prior to the interview or, if the elderly sample member had been institutionalized, in the month prior to his or her institutionalization.

Research interviewers administered interviews to the caregivers either in person or by telephone. Of the total of 2,503 elderly persons in the caregiver study, completed caregiver interviews were obtained for 1,940 individuals who met the study definition of an informal caregiver (see table 2–1).[8] The 1,940 completed interviews were fairly evenly spread across the ten study sites, with most sites contributing approximately 150 to 200 cases (see table 2–2). Miami and Philadelphia were represented more heavily, with 232 and 328 completed interviews, respectively.

Most caregiver interviews (67.1 percent) were completed by telephone; 32.3 percent were conducted in person, and less than 1 percent were administered through a combination of telephone and in-person efforts. After the elderly care recipient's own interview was completed, up to 45 days were allowed for completing the caregiver interview, although the average elapsed time between the elderly care recipient's interview and the date of the caregiver interview (or other final status) was

Table 2–1
Interviewing Results

Interviewing Result	Number	Percent
No appropriate caregiver named	274	10.9
Caregiver named but not interviewed:		
Refused to be interviewed	45	1.8
Not interviewed for other reasons	203	8.1
Interviewed but not appropriate, or another		
caregiver named but not interviewed	41	1.6
Appropriate caregiver named and interviewed	1,940	77.5
Total elderly in caregiver study	2,503	100.0[a]

[a]Does not add to 100.0 percent due to rounding error.

only 10.6 days. A small number of caregivers may have been interviewed after the elderly care recipient had begun to receive channeling services.[9] To that extent, the caregiver interview does not provide pure "baseline," or preintervention, data. However, all caregiver data were collected early in the period after the elderly care recipient had applied to the demonstration.

Summary and Overview of Book

This book is based on one of the several technical reports prepared for the channeling demonstration evaluation (Christianson and Stephens 1984). The report described the functioning of the informal care network for elderly participants prior to their receiving channeling services, so as to provide a context for understanding the impacts of channeling on informal caregiving. The goal of this book, which is also based on data from the baseline survey of informal caregivers, is to extend the existing knowledge about the characteristics and activities of family members and friends who regularly provide care to the impaired elderly.

In several ways, the data obtained from the channeling survey of primary informal caregivers respond to many of the methodological limitations with previous studies:

A large number of elderly persons and their caregivers were included in the study.

The elderly in the study were geographically dispersed—they included residents from ten communities across the nation, including both urban and rural areas, and persons of various ethnic and social backgrounds.

Table 2–2
Caregiver Study Sample Size and Interviewing Results, by Site

Site	Total Elderly in Caregiver Study	No Appropriate Caregiver Named		Caregiver Named but Not Interviewed		Appropriate Caregiver Named and Interviewed[a]	
		Number	Percent	Number	Percent	Number	Percent
Baltimore	221	11	5.0	29	13.1	181	81.9
Cleveland	241	11	4.5	52	21.6	178	73.8
Eastern Kentucky	200	21	10.5	28	14.0	151	75.5
Greater Lynn, Mass.	206	17	8.2	12	5.8	177	85.9
Houston	252	48	19.0	10	4.0	194	77.0
Miami	355	85	23.9	38	10.7	232	65.4
Middlesex County, N.J.	246	17	6.9	35	14.2	194	78.9
Philadelphia	436	54	12.4	54	12.4	328	75.2
Rensselaer County, N.Y.	179	2	1.1	19	10.6	158	88.3
Southern Maine	167	8	4.8	12	7.2	147	88.0
Total	2,503	274	10.9	289	11.5	1,940	77.5

[a]These cases are included in the caregiver study dataset.

All of the elderly were identified as at risk of institutionalization and were referred to the project for assessment and service coordination.

Survey data for both the elderly and their primary informal caregivers were obtained.

A particular individual was identified as the elderly person's primary informal caregiver on the basis of the care provided; primary caregivers were not restricted to particular relationships or to the provision of particular types of care for their inclusion in the study.

Information on informal caregiving was collected both for the primary informal caregiver and for the entire informal-care network.

Detailed data were obtained on the types and amount of care provided (including both financial assistance and hands-on care), and on a number of aspects of the well-being of caregivers and the stresses and constraints associated with caregiving.

The descriptive information we present in this book can serve as the foundation for developing more refined scientific hypotheses about and more precise policy objectives for informal caregiving. It is inevitable, however, that an analysis of any particular dataset will not be able to address all issues of interest, and that a number of questions must remain unanswered. In this case, it is important to recognize that the data from the channeling demonstration are not drawn from a representative sample of the nation's elderly (even its frail elderly), nor of their caregivers. The persons in this study came to one of the ten channeling projects at a critical juncture, often at a time when the elderly individual was being discharged from a hospital or when existing supports were no longer able to provide all of the care necessary for the elderly person. Therefore, drawing exact projections of the caregiving experiences to the nation as a whole is inadvisable. However, this limitation is also true of virtually every other study of informal caregiving. And, for some purposes, concentrating on the informal care provided to those elderly who are most at risk of institutionalization and who need a greater degree of assistance to remain in the community is more policy-relevant than describing the caregiving experiences for a more representative but less impaired group.

The data available from the channeling study enable us to examine five major topics, which are the subjects of the remaining chapters. Chapter 3 describes the demographic, economic, and social characteristics of both the elderly participants in the channeling demonstration and their caregivers. In particular, the living situations and impairment levels of the elderly care recipients are described, as are the relationship between the caregivers and care recipients and the age, health, family status, and employment experiences of the caregivers.

Chapter 4 focuses on the services provided by the primary informal caregivers. This chapter disaggregates assistance with personal care into specific tasks: eating, getting out of bed or a chair, dressing, bathing, toileting, and cleaning up after bowel or bladder accidents. Details are also provided on help with medical care, as well as on several household tasks, supervision for personal safety, and socialization. Chapter 4 also reports the frequency with which different types of care are provided by primary caregivers, as well as the time they devote to delivering care.

Chapter 5 expands the focus of the discussion to include the total caregiving network. It reports the number of caregivers in the caregiving network, examines the composition of this network, and describes the particular services delivered: personal care; meal preparation; housework and laundry, chores, or shopping; assistance in administering medicines, medical treatments, or therapies; transportation; money management; supervision for personal safety; and socialization. In addition, the time devoted by the informal caregiving network to delivering services is also estimated.

Chapter 6 addresses the amount of the financial assistance provided informally and the characteristics of those who provide it. Expenditures on elderly recipients are examined by the size and characteristics of the financial assistance network, and the expenditures of the primary caregivers themselves are discussed vis-à-vis both their relationship to the care recipient and their living arrangements.

Chapter 7 identifies a variety of employment and social constraints experienced by caregivers, including restrictions on their privacy and social lives and on the time they spend with their families. The chapter also documents the prevalence of the types of care recipient behavior that are considered to be problems for caregivers, and presents data on the satisfaction of caregivers with available care, their concern about the availability of care alternatives, and their assessment of the likelihood of institutionalization for the care recipient. The chapter concludes by presenting the responses of caregivers to a series of questions on the emotional, physical, and financial strain of caregiving and on their general level of satisfaction with life.

Notes

1. Some elderly persons were residing in hospitals or nursing homes at the time of their application to channeling; however, medical and other professional staff had to certify that the elderly person would be discharged into a community setting within three months.

2. The six ADL activities were bathing, dressing, toileting, getting out of bed or a chair, continence, and eating.

3. The seven IADL activities were housekeeping, shopping, preparing meals, taking medicine, traveling, using the telephone, and managing finances. For the IADL eligibility criterion, the first two and the last three IADL activities were aggregated into two categories. Thus, applicants could qualify under four possible IADL areas.

4. While all channeling clients received these seven components, additional features of the demonstration divided clients into two groups: the *basic case management model* group and the *financial control model* group. The basic case management model relied primarily on the seven components to achieve its aims. The financial control model expanded service coverage for a core set of community services, including skilled nursing, therapy and home health, personal care, homemaking, meals, transportation, and others. It also established a funds pool that combined funds from various sources to ensure that services could be allocated on the basis of need rather than on the basis of the eligibility requirements of specific programs. The financial control sites required that, in addition to meeting the other eligibility criteria, elderly applicants for channeling services be eligible for Medicare Part A.

5. The experimental design and the use of random assignment are described more fully in Kemper et al. (1982).

6. Both groups were interviewed at six and twelve months after their enrollment in the demonstration, and half of each group were also interviewed at eighteen months.

7. These caregivers were also interviewed at six and twelve months.

8. The overall response rate of named caregivers was 87 percent. Only 2 percent of the caregivers who were named by the elderly sample members refused to be interviewed. Another 9 percent were unable to be interviewed for other reasons, including their own illnesses or their inability to schedule the interviews within the 45 days allowed after the elderly sample member was interviewed. A further 2 percent of the caregiver interviews were incomplete because the caregiver who was initially named by the elderly person was inappropriate for the survey and a second named caregiver could not be interviewed. Appendix A compares the circumstances of the elderly care recipients whose caregivers responded to the survey with those whose caregivers did not. Only a few statistically significant differences were found.

9. As of May 1983, the average elapsed time between the completion of the interview and the initial receipt of services was 20.2 days.

3
The Elderly and Their Primary Caregivers

M any studies of informal caregiving have documented the composition of informal care networks, particularly the relationship between informal caregivers and the recipients of their care. The evidence on the relationship between caregivers and care recipients is consistent across a number of studies: most elderly who need assistance turn to family members, and many of these family supports are women—wives, daughters, and daughters-in-law (see Caro and Blank 1984; Soldo and Myllyluoma 1983; Brody 1981; Cantor 1983). And, while a number of studies have found that the elderly strongly desire to maintain their own independent households if possible (see Sussman 1977; Seelbach 1977; Wake and Sporakowski 1972), joint living arrangements with caregivers are not unusual, although these arrangements appear to be decreasing over time (Shanas 1979).

This chapter describes the elderly who participated in the channeling demonstration and their informal caregivers, whose experiences form the basis for this book. We will pay special attention to how these study members are similar to, or different from, those in other studies, since these similarities or differences are likely also to play an important role in explaining the caregiving experience.

The Elderly in the Study

As described in chapter 2, a subset of the elderly participants in the channeling demonstration was included in the study of informal caregiving. Almost three-quarters of the elderly persons in the caregiver study were white, female, and 75 years of age or older (see table 3–1). Two-thirds were unmarried at the time of their interview, and almost 40 percent lived alone. Although nearly all were covered under either Medicare or Medicaid, their ability to pay for regular living expenses was generally rather limited. The majority had a gross monthly income (in-

Table 3–1
Sociodemographic Characteristics of Elderly in Caregiver Study
(percent)

Characteristic of Elderly Person	Total	No Informal Caregiver Named	Informal Caregiver Named
Sex:**			
Female	71.6	80.7	70.5
Age:*			
65 to 74 years	27.9	35.0	27.0
75 to 79 years	20.8	20.8	20.9
80 to 84 years	22.7	20.1	23.0
Older than 84 years	28.5	24.1	29.1
Ethnic background:			
Black	23.2	18.2	23.8
Hispanic	4.0	3.3	4.0
White or other[a]	72.8	78.5	72.1
Marital status:**			
Now married	31.7	17.2	33.5
Not presently married	68.3	82.8	66.5
Living situation:**			
Alone	37.4	69.7	33.5
With spouse	30.9	17.2	32.6
With child	20.7	5.5	22.6
With others	11.0	7.7	11.4
Monthly income:*			
Less than $300	12.7	11.0	12.9
$300 to $499	41.1	48.5	40.2
$500 to $999	35.6	34.3	35.8
$1,000 or more	10.6	6.2	11.2
Insurance coverage:			
Medicaid	20.8	24.4	20.4
Medicare, no Medicaid	78.2	74.8	78.6
Other	1.0	0.7	1.0

Note on statistical significance: Significance tests were based on the chi-square statistic for cross-tabulations. Significant differences between the distributions in columns 2 and 3 are denoted by asterisk(s) at the relevant characteristic: *denotes statistical significance at the 95 percent level; **denotes statistical significance at the 99 percent level.

[a]Other includes native Americans, Alaskan natives, Asians, or Pacific Islanders (totaling less than 1 percent of the sample).

cluding the incomes of their spouses and other household members) of less than $500; over 12 percent had incomes of less than $300 per month.

The elderly persons in the study were quite impaired (see table 3–2). Depending upon the specific task, up to three-quarters of the elderly were impaired in their ability to perform activities of daily living (ADL). Bathing was a task with which many experienced difficulty and required assistance. About half experienced problems in dressing, getting in and out of bed or a chair ("transfer"), and getting to and using the toilet. About one-quarter were unable to feed themselves without some assis-

Table 3–2
Impairment of Elderly in Caregiver Study
(percent)

Characteristic of Elderly Person	Total	No Informal Caregiver Named	Informal Caregiver Named
Impairment of ADL:			
Eating**	24.8	9.8	26.7
Toileting**	54.3	31.0	57.2
Bathing**	76.5	59.1	78.6
Transfer**	49.5	26.3	52.4
Dressing**	57.7	32.8	60.7
Impairment in continence**	51.0	35.0	53.0
Impairment of IADL:			
Use of telephone**	52.3	29.4	55.1
Money management**	69.6	35.1	73.8
Traveling**	86.7	72.1	88.6
Housework	97.2	95.6	97.4
Meal preparation**	86.7	70.4	88.7
Shopping**	95.0	84.6	96.3
Taking medicine**	57.7	21.3	62.1
Impairment of mental ability:[a]**			
Severe	29.7	12.4	32.6
Moderate	38.7	39.7	38.6
Mild	31.6	47.9	28.8

Note on statistical significance: Significance tests were based on the chi-square statistic for cross-tabulations. Significant differences between the distributions in columns 2 and 3 are denoted by asterisk(s) at the relevant characteristic: * denotes statistical significance at the 95 percent level; ** denotes statistical significance at the 99 percent level.

[a]Measured by the Short Portable Mental Status Questionnaire (SPMSQ), a 10-question test of mental functioning. Severe impairment was indicated by zero to five correct answers out of ten possible, moderate impairment by six to eight correct answers, and mild impairment by nine to ten correct answers.

tance. About half were incontinent, at least occasionally. The majority of the elderly persons were also impaired in their ability to perform household or instrumental activities of daily living (IADL) and in their cognitive functioning.

Compared with the general American population of persons 65 years of age or older (see U.S. Bureau of the Census 1983, 4), this group of elderly persons was ethnically and racially more diverse (23 percent of the elderly were black, compared with 8 percent in the nation), included a larger proportion of females (by 32 percentage points), and was older (28.5 percent of the channeling study elderly were 85 years of age or older, compared with 9 percent in the general population over age 65). In particular, the elderly in the channeling study were quite impaired and needed assistance. In 1978, less than 1 percent of the noninstitutionalized elderly in the nation as a whole required assistance with eating (U.S.

Bureau of the Census 1983, 99); in the channeling study, almost 25 percent needed assistance in this area. From 2 to 3 percent of the nation's elderly needed assistance with toileting, dressing, or bathing; in the channeling study, the respective figures were 54 percent, 58 percent, and 77 percent.

However, even though the elderly in the channeling study were defined as a population at risk of institutionalization, only a small proportion (not quite 10 percent) were in nursing homes six months after entering the demonstration (Kemper et al. 1985).[1] It is very likely that, as has been found in other studies, institutionalization was resisted by these elderly, and that their informal support networks were a key factor in helping them to continue living in the community.

The Provision of Informal Assistance

As expected in light of other studies of the care received by the elderly population, most of the elderly in the channeling study named a friend or family member who regularly provided assistance to them. Only 11 percent of the elderly in the study either did not name any informal caregiver or named someone who did not meet the study criteria as outlined in chapter 2. This response by informal sources to the needs of the elderly is similar to the levels found in other studies. For example, a National Center for Health Statistics (1972, 24) study found that at least 80 percent of the elderly being cared for at home received some help from family members or others, and a General Accounting Office (1977, 20) study found that all but 13 percent of the elderly reportedly were able to turn to a relative or friend for help during an illness.

A number of statistically significant differences existed between elderly individuals who named informal caregivers and those who did not (see tables 3–1 and 3–2). Elderly persons who did not name an informal caregiver were more likely to be female, to be between the ages of 65 and 75, to be unmarried and living alone, and to have low monthly incomes. Although the difference is not statistically significant, the data also suggest that they were less often of minority (black or Hispanic) background. Although all of the elderly persons in the study were referred or applied to the channeling projects for services, and were to meet eligibility criteria on their level of functional impairment, those elderly who did not name informal caregivers were significantly less impaired than the elderly who named caregivers. This finding reinforces the conclusion reached in many other studies that informal sources of care are important in terms of mitigating the demands placed on the formal service system.

The Primary Informal Caregivers

As we noted in chapter 1, some of the most consistent findings from the literature on informal caregiving pertain to the persons who provide informal care and how they are related to the elderly care recipients. For example, in a study cited by Lewis et al. (1980, 2), 45 percent of the elderly individuals, when asked on whom they would rely for assistance in a series of health-related tasks, chose a relative. In a General Accounting Office study (1977, 20), 42 percent of all elderly who were receiving help at home were cared for by their children, 27 percent were aided by spouses, and a much smaller percentage received help from friends and neighbors. The importance of children as caregivers was also emphasized by Morris, Sherwood, and Gutkin (1981, IV–9), who found that 58 percent of the networks under study consisted of at least one child of the care recipient. Friends and neighbors appear to represent the most tenuous element of the informal care network; elderly turn to them for assistance primarily when family members are unavailable (Stoller and Earl 1983). Shanas (1979, 171, 173) summarized the evidence on the likely relationship between caregivers and care recipients as follows: elderly males are most likely to receive care from their spouses, and elderly females rely predominantly on children (usually female) who reside both within and outside their households. This observed difference between the sexes appears to be due to the longer average life span of women, in that elderly women (if ever married) often outlive their spouses. Therefore, the general caregiving scenario consists of a woman (often age 55 or over) as the primary provider of services to an older, female relative.

This scenario was also observed in the informal caregiving network in the channeling demonstration study. Most of the primary caregivers in the study were female, and approximately two-thirds were providing care to a female care recipient (see table 3–3). Very rarely (in only 4.4 percent of the caregiving situations) was a male caregiver providing care to a male recipient.

A large proportion of caregivers (about 40 percent) were themselves elderly (65 years of age or older); almost 15 percent were over the age of 75. Reflecting this age distribution, almost all primary caregivers (over 84 percent) reported that no children under age 15 were residing in their households, but about one of six primary caregivers had other long-term caregiving responsibilities in addition to those associated with the elderly person in the channeling study. Only 12 percent of the primary caregivers were not related to the elderly care recipient. Almost one-half of all primary caregivers were the children or children-in-law of the care recipients, and another one-quarter were spouses. Daughter–mother was the most common relationship between caregiver and care recipient, al-

Table 3–3
Characteristics of Primary Caregiver

Characteristic of Primary Caregiver	Percent
Gender:	
Female	73.2
Gender of caregiver and care recipient:	
Both female	48.7
Both male	4.4
Caregiver female, care recipient male	24.4
Caregiver male, care recipient female	22.4
Age:	
40 years or younger	12.1
41 to 54 years	23.2
55 to 64 years	24.8
65 to 75 years	25.0
Older than 75 years	14.9
Ethnic background:[a]	
Black	23.8
Hispanic	3.7
White or other	72.4
Education completed:	
No formal education	0.9
Elementary education	22.6
Some high school	16.4
High school	31.6
Some post–high school	15.6
College	6.9
Post-college	5.9
Caregiver living arrangements vis-à-vis care recipient:	
Lives with care recipient:	
Spouse	22.7
Nonspouse	33.8
Does not live with care recipient	43.5
Marital status:	
Spouse of care recipient	22.8
Currently married, but not spouse of care recipient	39.3
Not currently married	37.9
Any children under age 15	15.7
Relationship to care recipient:	
Spouse	22.7
Daughter	31.1
Son	11.1
Daughter-in-law	4.4
Sibling or sibling-in-law	7.3
Other[b]	23.3
Other long-term caregiving responsibilities	16.7

[a]All those of Hispanic origin are reported in that category; "other" includes native Americans, Alaskan natives, Asians, or Pacific Islanders (totaling less than 1 percent of the sample).

[b]Other includes 1 parent (0.1 percent of all caregivers), 10 sons-in-law (0.5 percent), 71 grandchildren (3.7 percent), 138 other relatives (7.1 percent), 225 friends or neighbors (11.6 percent), and 7 employees or volunteers who were friends of the care recipient prior to providing care (0.4 percent).

though this relationship accounted for less than one-third of all caregiving situations.

The age of many of the caregivers in the study was reflected not only in their other household and family responsibilities, but also in their economic situation and physical health. Almost two-thirds of the primary caregivers were not working at the time of their interview, and most of the caregivers who did not have jobs (which included those who had retired or had never worked outside the home) had not worked within the past year (see table 3–4). Of the caregivers who were currently employed, the large majority were working full time, and the earnings of caregivers who did have jobs generally represented a substantial share (half or more) of their total household income. Caregivers were generally financially better off than care recipients; almost 60 percent had gross monthly incomes of $1,000 or more. Because these results include the incomes of spouse caregivers, it is clear that nonspouse caregivers had substantially higher incomes than the elderly care recipients and their spouses.

Although the majority of the primary caregivers (60 percent) reported that their own general health was excellent or good, almost 13 percent stated that they were in poor health (see table 3–5). A relatively small proportion (not quite 12 percent) reported some limitation in their own ability to perform personal-care tasks (such as dressing, bathing, eating, or toileting), but a larger proportion (close to 28 percent) experienced problems with such instrumental tasks as meal preparation, housework, shopping, traveling, and similar activities. Fully 30 percent of the persons on whom the frail elderly care recipients relied for most of their informally provided care were experiencing health problems of sufficient severity to make their own lives difficult.

Summary

The nearly 2,000 caregivers interviewed in the channeling study were identified by the elderly care recipients as the family members or friends who provided the greatest amount of informal care; over 89 percent of the elderly in the demonstration named such a primary caregiver. Many of the primary caregivers were spouses or children of the care recipient, very often women. About one-third of the primary caregivers worked outside the home, and approximately one-sixth had other caregiving responsibilities. This profile of those who provide informal care to frail elderly persons is consistent with other previous studies, and supports the view that the care of the elderly is an integral component of the everyday lives of many middle-aged and older Americans.

The remaining chapters present information obtained from the pri-

Table 3–4
Income and Employment of Primary Caregiver

Characteristic of Primary Caregiver	Percent
All	
Monthly family income:[a]	
Less than $500	18.4
$500 to $999	23.6
$1,000 or more	58.0
Employment status:	
Currently employed	34.3
Employed within past year but not currently employed	7.1
Not currently employed, and not employed	
within past year	58.6
Currently employed[b]	
Hours worked per week:	
Part time (34 hours or less per week)	
Less than 20 hours per week	11.1
20 to 34 hours per week	18.0
Full time (35 hours or more per week)	
35 to 40 hours per week	53.2
More than 40 hours per week	17.7
Monthly earnings:[c]	
Less than $500	20.1
$500 to $999	23.4
$1,000 or more	56.6
Family income from caregiver earnings:	
25.0 percent or less	10.1
25.1 to 50.0 percent	18.4
50.1 to 75.0 percent	23.4
75.1 percent or more	48.2

[a]Family income was asked for the month prior to the interview month. Respondents were asked to report total family income, before taxes and other deductions, in categories. The midpoint of each category was then assigned, and missing data cases were assigned the mean of the reported values. Mean monthly family income, including imputed missing data, was $1,195 (n = 1,784); the mean, excluding imputed missing data, was $1,176 (n = 1,654).

[b]The number of currently employed caregivers was 663.

[c]Respondents were asked to report usual monthly earnings, before taxes and other deductions, in actual dollars. If unwilling or unable to provide actual dollar earnings, they were asked to report earnings in categories. Reports in categories were recoded to the mean value of actual dollar reports falling within those categories. The overall mean was assigned to missing data. Mean monthly earnings, including imputed missing data and data recoded from reports in categories, was $1,160 (n = 663); the mean, excluding imputed missing data, was $1,158 (n = 600); the mean for reports in actual dollars was $1,185 (n = 514).

mary informal caregivers in the channeling study on their own and others' experience in providing care and financial assistance to their elderly relatives or friends. Where appropriate, comparisons of the caregiving situation are drawn among subgroups defined by characteristics of the

Table 3–5
Health of Primary Caregiver

Characteristic of Primary Caregiver	Percent
Self-reported overall health:	
Excellent	20.8
Good	38.6
Fair	27.7
Poor	12.9
Limitations in functional capacity:[a]	
No problems with either ADL or IADL tasks	69.7
Some problems with IADL, but not ADL, tasks	18.7
Some problems with ADL, but not IADL, tasks	2.4
Some problems with both ADL and IADL tasks	9.2

[a]ADL limitations include problems with eating, getting out of bed or a chair, dressing, bathing, or using the toilet. IADL limitations include problems with preparing meals, doing housework, shopping or doing chores, taking medicine, traveling more than walking distance, managing money, or using the telephone.

caregivers. Based on the findings from previous studies, the two key characteristics selected for these comparisons are the caregiver's relationship to the care recipient and whether or not the two live in the same household.

Notes

1. Of course, some additional proportion of the elderly may have entered nursing homes and subsequently died during that six-month period; however, the relative rarity of this situation would not have greatly increased the total rate of institutionalization.

4

Care by Primary Informal Caregivers

As we reported in the previous chapter, most of the elderly in the channeling demonstration study received regular care from informal sources. The individuals named by the elderly as the friend or family member who provided the greatest amount of assistance are central to an understanding of informal caregiving. This chapter examines in detail the care provided by these primary informal caregivers. Its purpose is to describe the types and level of informal care provided to the frail elderly and how caregiving responds to the circumstances of the caregiver.

Types of Care Provided by Primary Informal Caregivers

In summarizing the literature on informal caregiving activities, Dunlop (1980, 515) concludes that the informal care provided in the home generally entails day-to-day housework and personal attention, rather than nursing care. For example, as was found in a General Accounting Office (1977) study conducted in Cleveland, personal care is most often provided by families, and, as noted by Frankfather, Smith, and Caro (1981, 34), family members frequently provide light housekeeping and personal care, but provide help with heavy housekeeping and home repair only on a relatively infrequent basis, as expected from the nature of these tasks. Although the Frankfather, Smith, and Caro study also reported that administering medicine is one of the tasks that is most frequently undertaken by informal caregivers, other studies concluded that families generally do not take on such medical-care tasks as administering medication, checking blood pressure, or assisting with the use of a catheter (see General Accounting Office 1977).

Primary caregivers in the channeling study were asked whether they provided each of fifteen specific types of in-home care, which fall into four major categories: medical care, personal care, help with instrumental activities of daily living (IADL) and other care tasks, and staying with the elderly person because he or she requires supervision for personal safety and should not be left alone. Supervision over personal-care tasks, medical-care tasks, and the administration of medication—that is, by staying in the same room to offer assistance to ensure that these tasks are properly carried out—is also counted as caregiving for those tasks. When reporting each type of care, caregivers were asked to include only that care which is provided regularly—that is, on a routine basis at least once a month.[1]

Primary caregivers were asked to supply specific details on the types of personal, household, and medical care they provided. Personal care included the following tasks:

1. Feeding the elderly care recipient or helping him or her eat, excluding cutting meat or buttering bread
2. Helping the elderly person out of bed or a chair
3. Helping the elderly person dress or change into nightclothes, by getting the clothes for or putting them on the person
4. Helping the care recipient bathe in a tub or shower, at a sink or basin, or in bed, including helping the person get in and out of the tub or shower
5. Helping the elderly person to get to or to use the toilet, including help with a bedside commode, catheter, colostomy bag, or diapers
6. Cleaning up after bladder or bowel accidents

Help with medical care included assistance with physical, occupational, or speech therapy (including the supervision of exercises), and help with other medical treatments, such as giving oxygen or changing bandages. IADL and other in-home care included the following tasks:

1. Administering medicine or giving injections
2. Fixing meals or preparing special meals
3. Doing laundry or day-to-day housework around the home
4. Shopping for food, clothing, or other items
5. Doing chores, such as washing windows or making minor repairs
6. Helping to manage the care recipient's money, by writing checks or paying bills (but not including the provision of direct financial support, which is discussed in chapter 6)

Primary informal caregivers also described their involvement in two types of care regularly provided outside the home—help with transportation and help in finding out about or arranging for services or benefits on behalf of the care recipient. Finally, caregivers were asked whether they spent any time "socializing" or keeping company with care recipients, independent of the time they actually devoted to providing care.

The types of care provided by informal caregivers in the channeling study generally confirm the findings of previous research. Of the categories of in-home care provided to elderly care recipients, medical care was the least frequently mentioned by the primary caregivers in the channeling study (see table 4–1). In contrast, almost all primary caregivers provided help with at least one IADL or other household task. Almost 90 percent helped with shopping, nearly 80 percent with meals and

Table 4–1
Types of Care Provided by Primary Caregiver

Type of Care	Percent Providing Care
In-home care	
Medical care:	
Help with therapy (physical, occupational, speech)	14.3
Other medical treatments	10.7
Any medical care	21.7
Personal care:	
Help with eating	22.3
Help with getting out of chair or bed	45.2
Help with dressing	52.8
Help with bathing	46.2
Help with toileting	39.8
Cleaning up after bowel, bladder accidents	39.0
Any personal care	71.0
IADL or other care:	
Help with taking medicine	58.9
Meal preparation	79.1
Housework and laundry	77.9
Shopping	87.7
Chores	55.3
Managing money	74.5
Any IADL or other care	98.9
Supervision for personal safety	41.5
Any in-home care[a]	99.1
Services produced outside the home	
Transportation	51.6
Arranging Services	59.1
Socializing (keeping company)	81.8

[a]All primary caregivers provided some regular care to the elderly care recipients, although not all provided in-home care.

housework, and almost 75 percent with managing money. Help with medications and help with chores were less frequently mentioned, but were still provided by over half of the primary caregivers. Personal care was also provided frequently—more than 70 percent of the primary caregivers performed at least one personal care task, over 50 percent provided help with dressing, and a somewhat smaller percentage helped with bathing and getting out of bed or a chair. The type of personal care least frequently provided was help with eating (22 percent of the caregivers reported providing this assistance). Almost 40 percent of the caregivers helped regularly with toileting and with problems associated with incontinence. Slightly more than 40 percent provided supervision for personal safety. Help with transportation and with arranging for services and benefits was provided by more than half of the caregivers. The majority of caregivers helped with more than one caregiving task, and over 80 percent kept company with the care recipient above and beyond the time they devoted to other caregiving tasks.

Previous studies suggest that both the relationship with the elderly care recipient and whether the caregiver lives with the recipient are significant factors in the types of care provided by informal caregivers. Lewis et al. (1980, 6) concluded that spouses and children are much more likely than other relatives or friends to engage in such activities as meal preparation, grocery shopping, and trips to the doctor. In addition, Cantor's research (1980) suggested that the children of moderately disabled care recipients are the most likely of all caregivers to provide help with shopping, transportation to medical care, financial management, meal preparation, and home repair. Treas (1977, 488) observed that a sexual division of labor among family caregivers often exists in terms of whether and what types of assistance are provided to elderly persons, and cited studies which found that sons are involved primarily in managing financial matters and making funeral arrangements, while daughters provide a broader spectrum of support services. Caro and Blank (1984) also reported that daughters often represent key informal supports. Evidence from other studies (see summary in Shanas 1979) point out that spouses, most often wives, provide the most comprehensive informal care of all informal supports, both because of their availability in the home and because of the intensity of their relationship.

These patterns were generally confirmed by the channeling data. Although virtually all primary caregivers in the channeling study provided some type of in-home care, spouses were more likely than other caregivers to provide personal care, medical care, most other types of in-home care, and supervision for personal safety than were other caregivers (see table 4–2). However, spouses were less likely than other primary caregivers to help with chores, shopping, transportation, or arranging for

Table 4–2
Types of Care Provided by Primary Caregiver, by Relationship to Care Recipient
(percent providing care)

				Relationship to Care Recipient			
Type of Care	*All Caregivers*	*Spouse*	*Daughter*	*Son*	*Daughter-in-law*	*Sibling[a]*	*Other*
In-home care							
Medical care:							
Help with therapy (physical, occupational, speech)**	14.3	20.2	18.1	9.3	15.1	12.0	6.4
Other medical treatments**	10.7	11.8	15.1	6.5	10.5	7.8	6.6
Any medical care**	21.7	28.2	27.7	14.4	22.1	17.6	12.0
Personal care:							
Help with eating**	22.3	32.7	26.3	19.1	23.3	19.0	9.1
Help with getting out of chair or bed**	45.2	56.4	52.0	39.5	41.9	34.5	32.1
Help with dressing**	52.8	70.5	62.9	28.5	58.1	43.7	35.2
Help with bathing**	46.2	64.2	58.8	16.7	50.0	38.7	27.4
Help with toileting**	39.8	55.8	46.5	29.8	44.2	32.4	21.7
Cleaning up after bowel, bladder accidents*	39.0	56.1	43.4	26.5	50.6	29.1	23.2
Any personal care**	71.0	90.3	80.1	55.1	67.4	64.8	50.0
IADL or other care:							
Help with taking medicine**	58.9	78.5	66.9	52.3	64.0	50.7	33.8
Meal preparation**	79.1	94.8	84.8	61.2	90.7	78.2	62.6
Housework and laundry**	77.9	91.2	85.6	66.8	83.7	73.9	60.1
Shopping**	87.7	85.5	91.9	89.3	91.9	81.7	84.5
Chores**	55.3	59.2	59.2	73.7	59.3	35.5	43.0
Managing money**	74.5	92.1	78.6	79.5	61.6	66.2	54.3
Any IADL or other care	98.8	99.8	99.5	96.7	100.0	100.0	97.1
Supervision for personal safety**	41.5	57.7	48.6	32.2	43.0	38.0	21.3
Any in-home care	99.1	100.0	99.5	98.1	100.0	100.0	97.6

Table 4–2 continued

Type of Care	All Caregivers	Relationship to Care Recipient					
		Spouse	Daughter	Son	Daughter-in-law	Sibling[a]	Other
Services produced outside the home							
Transportation**	51.6	41.2	58.1	66.0	58.1	39.0	48.8
Arranging Services**	59.1	52.4	68.8	66.0	75.6	47.9	49.8
Socializing (keeping company)	81.8	85.2	81.3	79.1	73.3	83.0	81.6

Note on statistical significance: Significance tests were based on the chi-square statistic for cross-tabulations. Significant differences among entries in columns 2 through 7 are denoted by asterisks at the relevant type of care: ** denotes statistical significance at the 99 percent level.
[a]Includes siblings-in-law.

services and benefits. These types of services were performed more often by the children of the care recipient.

Among nonspouse caregivers, daughters and daughters-in-law were especially likely to provide personal care, medical care, and other in-home care (such as help with medicine, meal preparation, and housework), as is consistent with the literature on informal caregiving. Sons who were primary caregivers were less likely than daughters or daughters-in-law to provide most types of in-home care. However, they were the most likely of all primary caregivers to provide transportation assistance and help with chores. Siblings and more distant kin and friends (the category labeled as "Other" in table 4–2) were generally the least likely of all caregivers to provide each type of in-home care or care outside the home. However, no differences by relationship existed in terms of whether time was devoted to keeping company or socializing with the care recipient.

In comparing the types of care provided by male and female primary caregivers to elderly men and women regardless of their relationship to each other, we find further evidence of the sexual division of labor in caregiving. Female caregivers, regardless of whether they are helping male or female elderly persons, were more likely than male caregivers to provide personal care, medical care, and most other types of help with daily household tasks (see table 4–3). Male caregivers—generally husbands and sons—were more likely to provide help with traditionally "male" activities, such as heavy chores and transportation.

Previous studies have also documented that more care is provided by caregivers who live with the elderly care recipient. While the proportion of shared living arrangements seems to have decreased over time (see Shanas 1979), studies have found that elderly persons who live with their families generally need and receive more informal assistance (see, for example, Soldo and Myllyluoma 1983). This finding was dramatically demonstrated among primary caregivers in the channeling study, but, as might be expected, only for in-home services. About two times more caregivers who lived with care recipients provided personal, medical, and other in-home care than caregivers who did not live with care recipients (see table 4–4). Moreover, both live-in caregivers who were the spouse of the care recipient and other live-in caregivers were equally likely to provide the same types of care. However, caregivers who did not live with the care recipient were more likely to provide transportation services, and nonspouse caregivers, regardless of living arrangement, more often provided help in arranging for services or benefits.

The results of the channeling study confirm and expand upon those of previous studies: informal caregiving is concentrated more heavily in the provision of personal care and assistance in everyday household tasks

Table 4–3
Types of Care Provided by Primary Caregiver, by Gender of Caregiver and Care Recipient
(percent providing care)

Type of Care	All Caregivers	Gender of Caregiver and Care Recipient			
		Both Females	Both Males	Caregiver Female, Care Recipient Male	Caregiver Male, Care Recipient Female
In-home care					
Medical care:					
Help with therapy (physical, occupational, speech)	14.3	13.9	11.8	17.1	12.4
Other medical treatments	10.7	11.4	8.2	12.5	7.6
Any medical care*	21.7	21.5	17.6	26.0	18.1
Personal care:					
Help with eating**	22.3	21.4	10.6	27.5	20.7
Help with getting out of chair or bed*	45.2	44.1	32.9	49.3	45.6
Help with dressing**	52.8	55.7	25.9	64.5	38.8
Help with bathing**	46.2	51.6	25.9	54.3	29.5
Help with toileting**	39.9	39.9	20.0	45.0	38.0
Cleaning up after bowel, bladder accidents**	39.0	36.5	27.1	52.3	32.3
Any personal care**	71.0	70.8	47.1	80.3	65.8
IADL or other care:					
Help with taking medicine**	58.9	55.4	41.2	71.7	56.1
Meal preparation**	79.1	78.2	53.6	92.2	71.7
Housework and laundry**	77.9	77.6	58.3	89.2	70.0
Shopping	87.7	88.9	85.9	85.2	88.0
Chores*	55.3	48.1	63.9	53.0	71.9
Managing money**	74.5	69.3	63.5	80.6	81.3
Any IADL or other care	98.8	99.2	97.6	98.5	98.4
Supervision for personal safety**	41.5	41.1	22.4	48.5	38.3
Any in-home care	99.1	99.2	98.8	98.9	99.1

Services produced outside the home

Transportation**	51.6	53.3	60.0	40.6	58.3
Arranging services	59.1	61.6	56.5	55.1	58.7
Socializing (keeping company)	81.8	82.5	81.2	79.7	82.6

Note on statistical significance: Significance tests were based on the chi-square statistic for cross-tabulations. Significant differences in distributions among columns 2 through 5 are denoted by asterisk(s) at the relevant type of care: * denotes statistical significance at the 95 percent level; ** denotes statistical significance at the 99 percent level.

Table 4–4

Types of Care Provided by Primary Caregiver, by Living Arrangement
(percent providing care)

Type of Care	All Caregivers	Lives with Care Recipient		Does Not Live with Care Recipient
		Spouse	Nonspouse	
In-home care				
Medical care:				
Help with therapy (physical, occupational, speech)**	14.3	20.2	19.7	7.0
Other medical treatments**	10.7	11.9	15.3	6.5
Any medical care**	21.7	28.3	29.3	12.3
Personal care:				
Help with eating**	22.3	32.8	31.6	9.6
Help with getting out of chair or bed**	45.2	56.3	60.2	27.8
Help with dressing**	52.8	70.4	70.3	29.9
Help with bathing**	46.2	64.1	62.4	24.3
Help with toileting**	39.8	55.7	55.8	19.2
Cleaning up after bowel, bladder accidents**	39.0	56.3	52.8	19.3
Any personal care**	71.0	90.2	88.0	47.7
IADL or other care:				
Help with taking medicine**	58.9	78.6	79.3	32.7
Meal preparation**	79.1	94.8	93.6	59.6
Housework and laundry**	77.9	91.1	91.9	60.1
Shopping**	87.7	85.4	91.5	85.9
Chores**	55.3	59.3	69.7	42.0
Managing money**	74.5	92.3	78.8	61.8
Any IADL or other care	98.8	99.8	99.7	97.5
Supervision for personal safety**	41.5	57.9	61.7	17.2
Any in-home care	99.1	100.0	99.7	98.1
Services produced outside the home				
Transportation**	51.6	41.1	50.3	58.0
Arranging services**	59.1	52.3	63.2	59.5
Socializing (keeping company)	81.8	85.1	84.9	77.6

Note on statistical significance: Significance tests were based on the chi-square statistic for cross-tabulations. Significant differences among entries in columns 2 through 4 are denoted by asterisks at the relevant type of care: ** denotes statistical significance at the 99 percent level.

than in the provision of medical or nursing care, even for this quite disabled group of elderly. Caregivers who are closely related to the elderly person are involved in a greater number of caregiving tasks, particularly in household tasks and in personal and medical care. Spouses and others who live with the care recipient are especially likely to provide in-home care. Women (wives, daughters, and daughters-in-law) generally take on the more intimate daily tasks of caregiving, and men provide more help with tasks that are less emotionally burdensome, that are traditionally male-oriented, and that by their nature are less frequently necessary.

Frequency and Hours of Care

While the importance of both informal supports to caring for the elderly and the variety of types of assistance provided by informal caregivers is well documented, considerably less information is available on the amount of care being provided. Those studies that do provide data on the levels of informal care reinforce the importance of its contribution to the well-being of elderly individuals. For example, Horowitz and Dobrof (1982, 166, 169) reported that primary caregivers provide personal and health care on a regular basis, although only infrequently provide transportation assistance, another common area of informal care. Furthermore, all spouse primary caregivers in their study devoted more than 25 hours per week to providing care, while only 12 percent of the children and other relatives devoted as much time; indeed, 31 percent of the children and 45 percent of other relatives who were the primary caregivers devoted less than five hours per week to caregiving. Newman (1976), in a study of three-generation households that contained an elderly person in poor health, found that 40 percent of the middle-generation caregivers devoted more than 40 hours per week to caregiving activities. Finally, Paringer (1983, 22, 23)—using an algorithmic approach to estimate the hours of informal care provided to the elderly per week, based on data from the 1971 Manitoba Longitudinal Study on Aging—found that individuals whose ability to perform instrumental activities of daily living was limited received about nine hours of informal care per week, while those with limited mobility received an additional half-hour of care. Those individuals whose most severe limitation pertained to the area of grooming received an average of 14 hours of care; those who needed help in feeding and transfer received over 27 hours of care.

   Providing more information on the level of care is one area in which the channeling data make an important contribution to our knowledge of informal caregiving. Not only are data on the frequency and hours of care available in considerable detail, but the level of care that was provided represents something similar to an upper bound to the care available from primary informal caregivers. The elderly participants in the channeling demonstration were referred to the projects because of their unmet needs for assistance beyond what their existing, largely informal, service network could provide. As we shall see, this threshold for re-questing additional assistance is quite high.

The frequency of care in the channeling study was measured in two ways. First, caregivers were asked a general question to determine the number of days per week or month in which they provided any care. Then, for each type of personal and medical care provided by the care-giver, specific questions were asked to determine the number of times that each type of care was provided on an average day when the caregiver was helping.[2] This second, more specific set of questions captured the variation in the frequency with which care was provided for particular types of caregiving tasks. The frequency of caregiving was not asked for certain tasks—for instance, supervision for personal safety, socializing, and providing in-home care tasks other than help with medication (that is, meal preparation, housework, chores, shopping, and money manage-ment). Caregivers reported the frequencies of services provided outside the home (transportation and service arrangements) in terms of the num-ber of times per week or month; these responses were then converted into average daily frequencies.

The average daily frequency of care for each type of care was defined as the number of times the caregiver helped with the particular care task during the days when he or she helped, multiplied by the proportion of days per week the caregiver provided any help. The resulting measure is thus adjusted for the fact that not all caregivers helped every day.[3] Fre-quency of care by task was coded as zero if the caregiver did not provide that type of assistance.

Among all caregivers, only three caregiving tasks had a mean fre-quency of being provided once a day or more: help with getting out of bed or a chair, help with toileting, and help with medications (see table 4–5). On average, caregivers helped every other day with eating, bathing, and continence; the lower average frequency is due to the smaller num-bers of caretakers who provided any help with these tasks, and partic-ularly to the (expected) less frequent provision of help with bathing. The tasks that were performed rarely included help with transportation, with arranging for services or benefits, with physical or other therapy, and with administering other medical treatments.

Of course, caregivers who actually helped with each task did so more frequently than did caregivers in general, as is also shown in table 4–5. Caregivers who helped with getting out of bed or a chair did so almost four times a day on average, as did those who helped with toileting. These are tasks for which frequent help is expected if any is necessary at all. In contrast, tasks that required the least frequent assistance from caregivers were transportation and arranging for services. However, for most tasks, if caregivers provided any assistance, they generally did so more than once a day and often more than twice a day.

Table 4–5
Frequency of Care by Primary Caregiver
(mean number of times per day)

Type of Care	All Caregivers[a] Average Daily Frequency[b]	Caregivers Who Provided the Particular Type of Care	
		Average Daily Frequency	(Sample Size)
In-home care			
Medical care:			
Physical, occupational, or speech therapy	0.3	2.0	(273)
Administering other medical treatments	0.2	1.6	(204)
Personal care:			
Help with eating	0.6	2.6	(428)
Help with getting out of chair or bed	1.7	3.8	(855)
Help with dressing	0.8	1.5	(1,014)
Help with bathing	0.4	0.8	(888)
Help with toileting	1.4	3.7	(753)
Cleaning up after bowel, bladder accidents	0.6	1.6	(721)
IADL or other care:			
Help with taking medicine or giving injections	1.6	2.7	(1,133)
Services produced outside the home			
Transportation[c]	0.08	0.16	(995)
Arranging services	0.12	0.22	(1,005)

Note: Average daily frequency was coded as zero for caregivers who did not provide a particular type of care.

[a]The total number of caregivers with valid data was 1,940.

[b]Number of times in an average day when helping multiplied by the proportion of days providing any care in an average week.

[c]Round trips.

Primary informal caregivers were also asked to report the number of hours they devoted to providing assistance in three major categories of care: help with personal care, medications, and medical treatment; help with other tasks (meal preparation, housework or laundry, shopping, chores or minor repairs, transportation, and money management); and socializing (just keeping company) with the care recipient.

The responses of caregivers to questions on the time they devoted to care were given in terms of the hours of care they provided on a usual day when they did help, and were multiplied by the proportion of days during which the caregiver provided any help, to construct a measure of the average hours per day they devoted to providing care. The average hours per day were then summed over the three categories to provide a measure of the total time commitment of caregivers.

Primary informal caregivers provided an average of approximately two hours of care per day in each task category (see table 4–6). Among the caregivers who provided personal or medical care, they devoted an average of almost three hours per day to these tasks. The average time devoted to other caregiving tasks by caregivers who provided such help was only slightly over two hours—close to the figure for all caregivers, since virtually every caregiver provided some in-home care on tasks other than personal or medical care. The time devoted to socializing also averaged just over two hours per day, and was only slightly higher for caregivers who actually provided this type of care than for all caregivers. The average total time devoted by primary caregivers was 5.7 hours per day, which included socializing with the elderly person and providing assistance with personal and medical care and household tasks. Such activities represent a substantial time commitment by family and friends who provide care to the elderly.

As we mentioned earlier, the level of care provided by informal care-

Table 4–6
Time Devoted to Care by Primary Caregiver
(mean hours per day)

Type of Care	All Caregivers[a]	Caregivers Who Provided the Particular Type of Care	
	Average Hours per Day[b]	Average Hours per Day	(Sample Size)
Personal care, medical care, and help with taking medicine	2.0	2.8	(1,277)
Other tasks (over and above the time that would have been spent had the care recipient not been disabled)[c]	2.1	2.1	(1,660)
Socializing (keeping company)	1.8	2.2	(1,488)
Total time devoted to providing care[d]	5.7	—	—

Note: Hours per day was coded as zero for caregivers who did not provide a particular type of care.

[a]The total number of caregivers with valid data was 1,845.

[b]Hours in an average day when helping multiplied by the proportion of days providing any care in an average week.

[c]Includes meal preparation, laundry or housework, shopping, chores or minor repairs, transportation, and money management.

[d]Does not equal the sum of hours on separate tasks, due to incomplete data from some caregivers.

givers to the elderly in the channeling demonstration may well represent the maximum or threshold level beyond which informal caregivers need further assistance. On average, primary caregivers provided care almost every day and devoted an average of four hours per day to caregiving tasks, not including the time spent socializing with the elderly person. Most caregivers were involved in providing some assistance in personal care, and almost all helped with regular household tasks. This was the case despite the fact that the elderly in the demonstration were often receiving some formal community-based services prior to their applying for channeling. Depending upon the site, between 56 and 66 percent received formal in-home care, and between 15 and 18 percent received home-delivered meals (Kemper et al. 1985, 74, table 3–7).

Relationship, Living Arrangement, and Level of Care

Not all caregivers help to the same extent. In particular, the level or amount of caregiving is influenced by both the relationship of the caregiver to the care recipient and by their living arrangement vis-à-vis each other.

In terms of the frequency with which assistance was provided, primary caregivers who were spouses of the elderly care recipients generally provided personal and medical care more frequently than any other group of caregivers (see table 4–7). Daughters and daughters-in-law also performed these tasks relatively frequently; sons and the "other" group (more distant relatives and friends) did so less frequently. No differences by relationship existed in terms of the frequency with which transportation assistance was provided, although the younger generation (sons, daughters, and daughters-in-law) assisted more frequently in arranging for services and benefits.

The relationship of the primary caregiver to the care recipient is also an important factor in the amount of time devoted to providing care. Caregivers who were spouses of the elderly care recipients devoted more time than any other caregivers to providing each category of care (see table 4–8), but particularly to socializing or keeping company with the elderly. Spouse caregivers devoted substantial portions of their day to caregiving, averaging over six hours per day in assistance with personal and medical care and other household tasks—almost two and one-half hours per day more than daughters and daughters-in-law, who devoted the next largest amount of time (about four and one-half hours) to caregiving. Primary caregivers who were sons devoted slightly less than three hours per day; more distant relatives and friends devoted an average of just over two hours per day to caregiving tasks.

Table 4–7
Frequency of Care by Primary Caregiver, by Relationship to Care Recipient
(average daily frequency)

Type of Care	All Caregivers	Relationship to Care Recipient					
		Spouse	Daughter	Son	Daughter-in-law	Sibling[a]	Other
In-home care							
Medical care:							
Physical, occupational, or speech therapy**	0.3	0.5	0.3	0.1	0.5	0.2	0.1
Administering other medical treatments**	0.2	0.2	0.2	0.1	0.2	0.1	0.1
Personal care:							
Help with eating**	0.6	0.9	0.7	0.4	0.6	0.5	0.2
Help with getting out of chair or bed**	1.7	2.5	2.0	1.2	2.1	0.7	0.8
Help with dressing**	0.8	1.2	0.9	0.4	0.9	0.6	0.4
Help with bathing**	0.4	0.6	0.5	0.1	0.5	0.3	0.2
Help with toileting**	1.4	2.2	1.8	1.0	1.7	0.8	0.5
Cleaning up after bowel, bladder accidents**	0.6	0.9	0.7	0.2	1.1	0.4	0.3
IADL or other care:							
Help with taking medicine or giving injections**	1.6	2.5	1.7	1.1	1.8	1.3	0.7
Services produced outside the home							
Transportation[b]	0.08	0.08	0.09	0.09	0.09	0.06	0.06
Arranging services**	0.12	0.09	0.15	0.16	0.22	0.07	0.09

Note on statistical significance: Significance tests were based on the F-statistic for analysis of variance. Significant differences among entries in columns 2 through 7 are denoted by asterisks at the relevant type of care: ** denotes statistical significance at the 99 percent level.
[a]Includes siblings-in-law.
[b]Round trips per day.

Table 4–8
Time Devoted to Care by Primary Caregiver, by Relationship to Care Recipient
(average hours per day)

Type of Care	All Caregivers	Relationship to Care Recipient					
		Spouse	Daughter	Son	Daughter-in-law	Sibling[a]	Other
Personal care, medical care, and help with taking medicine**	2.0	3.1	2.3	1.2	2.5	1.5	0.9
Other tasks (over and above the time that would have been spent had care recipient not been disabled)[b]**	2.1	3.1	2.3	1.6	1.9	2.1	1.4
Socializing (keeping company)**	1.8	3.0	1.6	1.4	1.2	1.7	1.2
Total time devoted to providing care[c]**	5.7	9.0	6.0	4.2	5.6	5.3	3.3

Note: Hours per day and average hours per day are coded as zero for caregivers who did not provide each type of care.

Note on statistical significance: Significance tests were based on the F-statistic for analysis of variance. Significant differences among entries in columns 2 through 7 are denoted by asterisks at the relevant type of care: ** denotes statistical significance at the 99 percent level.

[a]Includes siblings-in-law.

[b]Includes meal preparation, laundry or housework, shopping, chores or minor repairs, transportation, and money management.

[c]Does not equal the sum of hours on separate tasks, due to incomplete data from some caregivers.

The primary caregiver's living arrangement vis-à-vis the elderly care recipient was also significantly related to the frequency and hours of care they provided. Live-in caregivers, whether or not the spouse of the care recipient, provided in-home care of all types considerably more often than did caregivers who were not living with the elderly person (see table 4–9). Live-in caregivers other than the spouse provided the most frequent amount of assistance in arranging for services. The frequency with which help with transportation was provided did not differ by living arrangements.

Caregivers who lived with care recipients, regardless of their relationship, provided approximately six hours of care per day (see table 4–10). Caregivers who did not live with the elderly person generally provided one hour or less of care per day in each task group, regardless of

Table 4–9
Frequency of Care by Primary Caregiver, by Living Arrangement
(average daily frequency)

Type of Care	All Caregivers	Lives with Care Recipient		Does Not Live with Care Recipient
		Spouse	Nonspouse	
In-home care				
Medical care:				
Physical, occupational, or speech therapy**	0.3	0.5	0.4	0.1
Administering other medical treatments**	0.2	0.2	0.2	0.1
Personal care:				
Help with eating**	0.6	0.9	0.9	0.2
Help with getting out of chair or bed**	1.7	2.5	2.5	0.6
Help with dressing**	0.8	1.2	1.1	0.3
Help with bathing**	0.4	0.6	0.6	0.2
Help with toileting**	1.4	2.2	2.2	0.4
Cleaning up after bowel, bladder accidents**	0.6	0.9	0.9	0.2
IADL or other care:				
Help with taking medicine or giving injections**	1.6	2.5	2.2	0.6
Services produced outside the home				
Transportation[a]	0.08	0.08	0.08	0.08
Arranging services**	0.12	0.09	0.15	0.11

Note on statistical significance: Significance tests were based on the F-statistic for analysis of variance. Significant differences among entries in columns 2 through 4 are denoted by asterisks at the relevant type of care: ** denotes statistical significance at the 99 percent level.

[a]Round trips per day.

Table 4–10
Time Devoted to Care by Primary Caregiver, by Living Arrangement
(average hours per day)

Type of Care	All Caregivers	Lives with Care Recipient		Does Not Live with Care Recipient
		Spouse	*Nonspouse*	
Personal care, medical care, and help with taking medicine**	2.0	3.1	3.0	0.6
Other tasks (over and above the time that would have been spent had the care recipient not been disabled)[a]**	2.1	3.1	2.8	1.2
Socializing (keeping company)**	1.8	3.0	2.3	0.8
Total time devoted to providing care[b]**	5.7	9.0	8.0	2.5

Note: Hours per day and average hours per day are coded as zero for caregivers who did not provide each type of care.

Note on statistical significance: Significance tests were based on the F-statistic for analysis of variance. Significant differences among entries in columns 2 through 4 are denoted by asterisks at the relevant type of care: ** denotes statistical significance at the 99 percent level.

[a]Includes meal preparation, laundry or housework, shopping, chores or minor repairs, transportation, and money management.

[b]Does not equal the sum of hours on separate tasks, due to missing data from some caregivers.

whether the task involved personal and medical care, other in-home tasks, or socializing. Caregivers in more intimate daily contact with the elderly care recipients and whose relationship with them carried the expectation of greater responsibility did in fact provide assistance with a wider range of tasks, provided assistance more often, and committed more hours to caregiving. However, it should be noted that both primary caregivers who were extended family members or friends and those who did not reside in the same household with the elderly care recipient also provided regular assistance (including socializing), averaging two or more hours per day.

Summary

Most primary informal caregivers of the elderly in the channeling study provided assistance with such household tasks as meal preparation, housework, shopping, and money management. Over 70 percent of the primary caregivers helped with at least one personal care task, and most also spent time socializing with the elderly care recipient. As expected, medical care was the least frequently provided type of care. These results on the prevalence of personal care contrast sharply with the finding by Horowitz and Dobrof (1982, 165) that only 33.5 percent of primary caregivers provide personal care. The difference between these results is particularly surprising, since the caregiver sample in the Horowitz and Dobrof study was restricted only to relatives, who generally provide a greater amount of care. A likely explanation for the difference is the greater level of impairment exhibited by the elderly in the channeling demonstration, compared with the elderly who were studied by Horowitz and Dobrof.

Primary caregivers who were the spouses of care recipients were the most likely of all caregivers to provide both personal care and many of the other care tasks necessary in the home. Daughters and daughters-in-law were also very likely to provide these types of care, whereas sons were more likely to help with chores and transportation. Live-in caregivers were more likely than caregivers who did not live with the care recipient to provide every type of care, with the exception of transportation assistance. This finding contrasts with the results of Morris, Sherwood, and Gutkin (1981, V-5), which suggested that certain other types of activities (grocery shopping and banking) are more often provided by someone who does not live with the care recipient.

Including those who provided no care for a given task, we estimate that, on average, primary informal caregivers helped elderly care recipients more than once a day with getting out of bed or a chair, toileting, and administering medicine, and about once every other day with other medical and personal care tasks. Assistance with personal and medical care averaged two hours per day among all informal caregivers. Adding that time to the time devoted to helping with other household tasks and keeping company with the elderly person, we estimate that primary caregivers spent an average of almost six hours per day with the care recipient. Converting this figure to a weekly basis, we estimate that caregivers in the channeling study spent an average of almost 40 hours per week with the care recipient and 28 hours in caregiving activities—a greater amount of time than was generally found in previous studies.

A finding that is consistent with other studies is the division of labor that exists between males and females within the family. Primary caregivers who were the spouses (usually the wives) of the elderly persons provided the greatest amount of informal care, and, among children of the care recipient who were named as the primary caregiver, daughters and daughters-in-law were much more active in providing care than were their male counterparts. However, in two specific task areas—chores and transportation assistance—sons provided more care than did other primary caregivers. Help with these tasks and others represented a significant time commitment by sons; on average, sons who were the primary caregivers devoted more than the equivalent of a half-time job (averaging 4 hours every day) to providing informal support and socializing with their disabled parent. Live-in caregivers, regardless of their relationship to the elderly person, were more likely to provide most types of care, to provide them more frequently, and to devote more time to providing care than were caregivers who did not live with the care recipient. These findings are generally consistent with those of other studies.

Thus far, we have focused on the assistance provided by the primary informal caregiver. These individuals show a high level of commitment to helping their elderly relative or friend remain in the community; on average, in providing assistance to and socializing with the care recipient, they devote the equivalent of a full-time job. In the next chapter, we place their effort within the context of the entire informal support network.

Notes

1. By definition, all primary caregivers provided care in at least one area or task.

2. If caregivers reported helping less than once a day, a follow-up question was asked of them about how often they did provide help. Responses were coded into the following three frequency categories: every 2 to 4 days, every 5 to 7 days or once a week, and less often. Each of these categories was then assigned a value representing the number of times per day on the average: every 2 to 4 days (.333), every 5 to 7 days or once a week (.143), and less often (.056).

3. The average frequency of providing any help was 0.8 times per day.

5
Informal Caregiving Networks

T
he primary informal caregiver—the person named by the elderly care recipient as providing the greatest amount of care on a day-to-day basis—is potentially only one member of a larger informal support network. This chapter describes these networks for the elderly in the channeling study who reported receiving informal care. As we shall see, despite the presence of others in the larger network, a single person often bears most of the burden of caregiving.

Size and Composition of the Informal Networks

Because the primary informal caregivers in the study were providing the greatest amount of informal care from the perspectives of the elderly care recipients, they were assumed to be reasonably knowledgeable about the entire caregiving network. As part of the interviews administered to them, they were asked to name up to four additional persons who provided informal care to the elderly person and to describe the care provided by those individuals. Most primary caregivers were able to provide information on the network; only 2.3 percent of the primary informal caregivers reported that they did not know whether any other persons regularly provided help to the elderly care recipient. Even so, the questions in the interview about the total caregiving network were less numerous and less detailed than were those about the activities of the primary caregiver him or herself, and questions that required essentially subjective answers (that is, about the effects of caregiving on the family and on personal life, and perceived stress or strain) were not asked of the primary caregivers about other caregivers.

By definition, all caregiving networks contain at least one member, the primary informal caregiver. In the study, close to 60 percent contained at least two members, but very few (about 10 percent) contained as many as four or five (see the first column in table 5–1). The primary

Table 5–1
Characteristics of Caregiving Network, by Care Recipient Age
(percent)

Network Characteristic	All Networks	Care Recipient Age			
		Under 75	75 to 79	80 to 84	85 and Over
Size of caregiving network:**					
One (primary informal caregiver only)	40.9	39.5	47.3	37.6	40.3
Two caregivers	31.6	30.1	27.4	31.4	36.2
Three to five caregivers	27.4	30.3	25.4	31.0	23.5
Average number of caregivers in network	1.99	2.03	1.90	2.10	1.94
Caregiving networks with:**					
Spouse only	12.6	17.1	17.7	8.7	8.0
Spouse and child(ren)ª	7.3	13.2	5.5	5.5	4.7
Spouse, children, and others	2.0	3.6	1.7	1.6	0.9
Spouse and others	3.2	5.8	3.0	2.3	1.9
Child(ren) only	30.7	18.0	28.6	30.8	43.4
Child(ren) and others	18.1	16.1	16.2	23.0	17.6
Others only	26.1	26.1	27.4	28.2	23.5
Caregiving networks with:**					
All caregivers of same generation as the care recipientᵇ	17.9	25.9	22.9	13.2	10.9
Some caregivers of same generation, some of other generations	17.4	27.4	16.7	15.0	10.7
No one in network of the same generation	64.6	46.6	60.4	71.8	78.4
Caregiving networks with:**					
No live-in caregiver	38.6	34.2	40.3	44.0	37.4
One live-in caregiver, spouse of care recipient	22.2	33.6	26.4	15.5	14.0
One live-in caregiver, other than spouse	26.2	19.8	22.4	28.0	33.4
More than one live-in caregiver	13.0	12.5	11.0	12.5	15.2

Note on statistical significance: Significance tests were based on the chi-square statistic for cross-tabulations. Significant differences in the distributions between columns are denoted by asterisk(s) at the relevant variable: * denotes statistical significance at the 95 percent level; ** denotes statistical significance at the 99 percent level.

ªIncluding children by marriage.

ᵇSpouse, sibling, or sibling-in-law.

informal caregivers reported that an average of two persons (including themselves) regularly provided informal assistance to the elderly care recipient. On average, the networks of older care recipients were the same size as those of younger care recipients (table 5–1), as was true of the caregiving networks of male and female elderly persons (table 5–2). As expected, the caregiving networks of care recipients who lived alone or only with their spouses were smaller than those of other elderly persons (table 5–3).

Table 5–2
Characteristics of Caregiving Network, by Care Recipient Gender
(percent)

| | | Care Recipient Gender | |
Network Characteristic	All Networks	Male	Female
Size of caregiving network:			
One (primary informal caregiver only)	40.9	43.2	40.0
Two caregivers	31.6	28.7	32.8
Three to five caregivers	27.4	28.1	27.1
Average number of caregivers in network	1.99	1.98	2.00
Caregiving networks with:**			
Spouse only	12.6	25.8	7.2
Spouse and child(ren)[a]	7.3	14.2	4.6
Spouse, children, and others	2.0	3.4	1.4
Spouse and others	3.2	5.9	2.2
Child(ren) only	30.7	18.8	35.5
Child(ren) and others	18.1	10.8	21.1
Others only	26.1	21.2	28.1
Caregiving networks with:**			
All caregivers of same generation as the care recipient[b]	17.9	29.9	13.1
Some caregivers of same generation, some of other generations	17.4	27.8	13.2
No one in network of the same generation	64.6	42.3	73.7
Caregiving networks with:**			
No live-in caregiver	38.6	27.4	43.1
One live-in caregiver, spouse of care recipient	22.2	44.3	13.2
One live-in caregiver, other than spouse	26.2	17.0	30.0
More than one live-in caregiver	13.0	11.3	13.7

Note on statistical significance: Significance tests were based on the chi-square statistic for cross-tabulations. Significant differences in the distributions between columns are denoted by asterisk(s) at the relevant variable: * denotes statistical significance at the 95 percent level; ** denotes statistical significance at the 99 percent level.
[a]Includes children by marriage.
[b]Spouse, sibling, or sibling-in-law.

Networks were divided into categories according to the specific relationship—spouse, child, or other—of caregivers to the elderly care recipient. In slightly over 30 percent of the networks, all caregivers were children (including those related by marriage), and children were present in almost 60 percent of the networks. Older care recipients and female recipients regardless of age relied more often on networks that consisted only of children than did younger persons and men taken as a group (see

Table 5–3
Characteristics of Caregiving Network, by Care Recipient Living Situation
(percent)

Network Characteristic	All Networks	Care Recipient Living Situation[a]			
		Alone	With Spouse	With Child	With Others
Size of caregiving network:**					
One (primary informal caregiver only)	40.9	41.6	46.9	34.3	35.9
Two caregivers	31.6	31.7	28.3	35.8	32.3
Three to five caregivers	27.4	26.7	24.8	29.9	31.8
Average number of caregivers in network**	1.99	1.95	1.89	2.11	2.15
Caregiving networks with:**					
Spouse only	12.6	0.2	39.3	0	0
Spouse and child(ren)[b]	7.3	0	22.5	0.6	0
Spouse, children, and others	2.0	0.2	5.7	0.4	0
Spouse and others	3.2	0	10.0	0	0.4
Child(ren) only	30.7	32.9	12.6	64.6	3.6
Child(ren) and others	18.1	21.1	4.7	32.5	17.3
Others only	26.1	45.7	5.2	1.7	78.6
Caregiving networks with:**					
All caregivers of same generation as the care recipient[c]	17.9	7.2	41.9	0.4	18.6
Some caregivers of same generation, some of other generations	17.4	6.4	37.2	5.2	19.6
No one in network of the same generation	64.6	86.4	20.9	94.4	61.8
Caregiving networks with:**					
No live-in caregiver	38.6	94.4	14.7	4.8	14.1
One live-in caregiver, spouse of care recipient	22.2	0	69.6	0	0
One live-in caregiver, other than spouse	26.2	5.3	6.0	62.3	68.6
More than one live-in caregiver	13.0	0.3	9.7	33.0	17.3

Note on statistical significance: Significance tests were based on the chi-square statistic for cross-tabulations. Significant differences in the distributions between columns are denoted by asterisk(s) at the relevant variable: * denotes statistical significance at the 95 percent level; ** denotes statistical significance at the 99 percent level.

[a]Time lapses between care recipient and caregiver interviews account for differences in reports of living situation.

[b]Includes children by marriage.

[c]Spouse, sibling, or sibling-in-law.

tables 5–1 and 5–2). Since women tend to outlive men, it necessarily follows that the networks of women are more likely than those of men to consist only of children. Spouses played a much less prominent role than children in informal care networks. In only 12.6 percent of all networks (about 30 percent of those with only one member) was a spouse the sole caregiver, although in the caregiving networks of the elderly who lived with their spouses the spouse generally played a major role or was in fact the only member (see table 5–3). Somewhat surprisingly, other relatives and nonrelatives played a major role in caregiving networks; over one-quarter of all networks contained only these members. Close to one-half of the networks included at least one caregiver who was not a spouse or child of the care recipient.

As expected in light of the composition of networks by relationship, most networks (close to two-thirds) contained no members who were of the same generation (spouse, sibling, or sibling-in-law) as the elderly care recipient. Slightly over 17 percent of the caregiving networks contained members of both the same and different generations. Members who were not of the same generation included children and grandchildren, as well as friends and neighbors.[1]

In almost 40 percent of all networks, no caregiver was living with the elderly care recipient. Of those networks that did contain a live-in member, most contained only one such caregiver, about half of whom were spouses. Only 13 percent of all networks contained more than one live-in caregiver.

Care Provided by the Informal Caregiving Network

In their role as informants on the total informal caregiving network, primary caregivers were asked to estimate for each *other* person in the network the total time per day which that person devoted to providing care on days when he or she was helping the elderly care recipient. This figure was then multiplied by the proportion of days per week that each caregiver helped the elderly care recipient, to obtain an estimate of the average time per day devoted to providing help. Unlike the time estimates that primary caregivers were asked to make for themselves (described in detail in chapter 4), the total time estimate included the time that would have been devoted by the other caregivers during the course of normal household routines, as well as the time devoted to providing the necessary care to the disabled elderly care recipient. For example, the estimate included the time normally devoted by wives to preparing meals on a regular basis or by husbands to shopping before their spouses became ill or disabled, as was the time devoted by caregivers to shopping for and preparing special foods that might now have been required because of illness. Thus, the total time estimates for the networks are likely to be somewhat overstated relative to the time estimates reported by primary caregivers for themselves.[2]

The types of care provided by the network can be divided into three major groups: in-home care, services produced outside the home, and socializing. In-home care includes the following:

1. Medical care (help with medical treatments or therapies)
2. Personal care (help with eating, getting out of bed or a chair, dressing, bathing, using the toilet, and cleaning up after bladder or bowel accidents)
3. Help with instrumental activities of daily living (IADL) and other care—meal preparation, day-to-day housework, laundry, shopping, chores such as washing windows or making minor repairs, and money management (by writing checks or paying bills for the care recipient, but not providing direct financial assistance)
4. Supervision for personal safety (staying with the elderly person because he or she could not be left alone)

Help with transportation (either driving the elderly person in a private vehicle or assisting him or her in the use of public transportation) is the one service produced outside the home for which information was obtained for the entire network. The time devoted to socializing—that is, the time spent with the elderly care recipient other than when actually engaged in direct caregiving, including just keeping company, sitting and talking, or watching television with the care recipient—was also obtained for the network.

In most networks, at least one person provided help in all areas of care, with the exception of supervision for personal safety, which was provided in somewhat less than half of the networks (see table 5–4).

Table 5–4
Types of Care, by Size of Network
(percent of networks)

		Size of Network		
Type of Care	All Networks	One	Two	Three +
In-home care				
Medical care:**				
No help from network	35.6	41.4	33.7	29.7
Help from one caregiver	45.6	58.9	39.1	33.1
Help from more than one				
caregiver	18.8	N.A.	27.2	37.2
Personal care:**				
No help from network	26.0	31.1	25.1	19.4
Help from one caregiver	45.2	68.9	34.2	22.4
Help from more than one				
caregiver	28.9	N.A.	40.7	58.3

Table 5–4 *continued*

Type of Care	All Networks	Size of Network		
		One	Two	Three+
IADL or other care:				
Meal preparation**				
No help from network	15.6	20.5	14.2	10.0
Help from one caregiver	55.3	79.5	44.8	31.2
Help from more than one				
caregiver	29.1	N.A.	41.0	58.8
Housework, laundry,				
shopping, chores:**				
No help from network	2.5	4.3	1.6	0.9
Help from one caregiver	53.8	95.7	33.1	15.0
Help from more than one				
caregiver	43.7	N.A.	65.3	84.0
Managing money:**				
No help from network	19.0	21.0	19.1	15.8
Help from one caregiver	69.4	79.0	64.0	61.3
Help from more than one				
caregiver	11.6	N.A.	16.9	22.9
Any IADL or other care:				
No help from network	0.8	1.5	0.3	0.2
Help from one caregiver	49.4	98.5	22.0	7.7
Help from more than				
one caregiver	49.8	N.A.	77.7	92.1
Supervision for				
personal safety:**				
No help from network	57.4	63.2	55.7	50.6
Help from one caregiver	21.6	36.8	12.5	9.4
Help from more than one				
caregiver	21.0	N.A.	31.8	40.0
Any in-home care:				
No help from network	0.5	0.8	0.3	0.2
Help from one caregiver	46.8	99.2	15.5	4.7
Help from more than one				
caregiver	52.7	N.A.	84.2	95.1
Services produced outside the home				
Transportation:**				
No help from network	43.7	50.0	41.0	37.2
Help from one caregiver	39.2	50.0	37.0	25.8
Help from more than one				
caregiver	17.1	N.A.	22.0	37.0
Socializing (keeping company)**				
No help from network	13.1	19.8	10.4	6.2
Help from one caregiver	42.2	80.2	19.9	11.3
Help from more than one				
caregiver	44.7	N.A.	69.7	82.5

Note on statistical significance: Significance tests were based on the chi-square statistic for cross-tabulations. Significant differences among the distributions in columns 2 through 4 are denoted by asterisks at the relevant type of care: ** denotes statistical significance at the 99 percent level.

N.A. = Not applicable.

The caregiving network was especially likely to provide assistance in meal preparation, housework, money management, and socializing. With the exception of money management, these types of care were also likely to be performed by more than one member of the network. Compared with the results that were presented in chapter 4, it is apparent that others in the caregiving network do not provide different types of care than are provided by the primary caregiver. This finding is not surprising given the small size of networks in general and the major role that the primary caregiver plays in them.

As expected, network size bears a strong relationship to whether care is provided and by how many persons. Networks that consisted only of one member were the least likely of all networks to provide help to the elderly person regardless of the category of care, and this difference by network size reached statistical significance for many categories of care (see table 5–4). Certain tasks (in particular, money management and help with medical care) were generally handled only by one person, even if more caregivers were available in the network. In networks that consisted of three or more members, these persons were especially likely to share caregiving responsibilities (that is, more than one person providing care) in the areas of housework, meal preparation, and personal care.

Networks that consisted solely of caregivers who were not part of the elderly person's immediate family were the least likely of all networks to provide any given type of care (see table 5–5). At the other extreme, networks in which the sole caregiver was the spouse of the recipient were considerably more likely to provide each type of care, except with supervision for personal safety and transportation assistance. When the network included both spouse and children as caregivers, more members tended to be involved in each task, compared with other networks that contained multiple members. Where a spouse shared caregiving responsibilities with someone other than a child, a division of labor appeared to exist within the network whereby the spouse (usually the wife) continued caregiving in the areas of personal and medical care, meal preparation, and money management, but shared such tasks as housework and supervision for personal safety with another member. Socializing was very often shared by multiple caregivers, regardless of their relationship to the care recipient, when more than one was available.

Networks in which at least one caregiver lived with the care recipient were much more likely than those which contained no live-in caregivers to provide assistance, particularly with personal care and household tasks (see table 5–6). The major exception was transportation assistance, which was provided most often by networks in which no caregiver lived with the care recipient. Networks which contained more than one live-in caregiver usually shared caregiving responsibilities for most tasks except

Table 5-5
Types of Care, by Composition of Network
(percent)

				Caregiving Networks with:				
Type of Care	All Networks	Spouse Only	Spouse and Children	Spouse, Children, and Others	Spouse and Others	Children Only	Children and Others	Others Only
In-home care								
Medical care:**								
No help from network	35.6	21.7	16.2	29.0	20.6	30.9	31.5	58.5
Help from one caregiver	45.6	78.3	52.1	44.7	66.7	48.6	31.2	31.8
Help from more than one caregiver	18.8	N.A.	31.7	26.3	12.7	20.5	37.2	9.7
Personal care:								
No help from network	26.0	11.1	7.8	13.2	4.8	26.2	21.0	45.1
Help from one caregiver	45.2	88.9	34.5	26.3	58.7	48.4	24.2	37.8
Help from more than one caregiver	28.9	N.A.	57.8	60.5	36.5	25.4	54.8	17.2
IADL or other care:								
Meal preparation:**								
No help from network	15.6	4.9	15.6	4.9	29.8	6.4	9.9	2.6
Help from one caregiver	55.3	95.1	60.0	44.4	49.4	55.6	34.4	36.8
Help from more than one caregiver	29.1	N.A.	24.4	50.7	20.8	38.1	55.7	60.5
Housework, laundry, shopping, chores:**								
No help from network	2.5	2.0	1.4	0.0	0.0	2.0	1.4	4.9
Help from one caregiver	53.8	97.9	24.6	13.2	38.1	61.3	21.3	59.5
Help from more than one caregiver	43.7	N.A.	73.9	86.8	61.9	36.6	77.3	35.6

Table 5–5 continued

Type of Care	Caregiving Networks with:							
	All Networks	Spouse Only	Spouse and Children	Spouse, Children, and Others	Spouse and Others	Children Only	Children and Others	Others Only
Managing money:**								
No help from network	19.0	6.6	5.6	10.5	9.5	16.5	16.5	35.2
Help from one caregiver	69.4	93.3	73.9	60.5	85.7	71.3	63.6	56.9
Help from more than one caregiver	11.6	N.A.	20.4	29.0	4.8	12.3	20.0	7.9
Any IADL or other care:								
No help from network	0.8	0.4	0.0	0.0	0.0	0.7	0.3	1.8
Help from one caregiver	49.4	99.6	13.4	5.3	31.8	56.6	12.5	58.1
Help from more than one caregiver	49.8	N.A.	86.6	94.7	68.2	42.7	87.2	40.1
Supervision for personal safety:**								
No help from network	57.4	48.0	35.9	42.1	33.3	55.6	54.8	75.9
Help from one caregiver	21.6	52.0	21.1	10.5	28.6	23.5	7.4	14.6
Help from more than one caregiver	21.0	N.A.	43.0	47.4	38.1	20.8	37.8	9.5
Any in-home care:								
No help from network	0.4	0.0	0.0	0.0	0.0	0.3	0.3	1.2
Help from one caregiver	46.8	100.0	9.9	0.0	19.0	55.3	6.8	56.5
Help from more than one caregiver	52.7	N.A.	90.1	100.0	81.0	44.4	92.9	42.3

Services produced outside the home

Transportation:**								
No help from network	43.7	53.3	49.3	42.1	57.1	38.0	31.8	50.8
Help from one caregiver	39.2	46.7	32.4	26.3	30.2	43.4	36.6	36.6
Help from more than one caregiver	17.1	N.A.	18.3	31.6	12.7	18.7	31.5	12.6
Socializing (keeping company)								
No help from network	13.1	14.3	9.2	0.0	12.7	16.1	8.5	14.2
Help from one caregiver	42.2	85.7	16.9	7.9	28.6	45.6	15.6	47.4
Help from more than one caregiver	44.7	N.A.	73.9	92.1	58.7	38.3	75.8	38.3

Note on statistical significance: Significance tests were based on the chi-square statistic for cross-tabulations. Significant differences among the distributions in columns 2 through 8 are denoted by asterisks at the relevant type of care: ** denotes statistical significance at the 99 percent level.

Note: Children include children by marriage.

N.A. = Not applicable.

Table 5–6
Types of Care, by Network Living Arrangement
(percent)

Type of Care	All Networks	Caregiving Networks with:			
		No Live-in Caregiver	One Live-in Caregiver, Spouse	One Live-in Caregiver, Other Than Spouse	More Than One Live-in Caregiver
In-home care					
Medical care:**					
No help from network	35.6	61.7	20.9	21.4	11.9
Help from one caregiver	45.6	25.9	70.2	60.1	32.5
Help from more than one caregiver	18.8	12.4	8.8	18.5	55.6
Personal care:**					
No help from network	26.0	51.4	9.8	12.2	6.0
Help from one caregiver	45.2	29.8	70.0	59.5	19.4
Help from more than one caregiver	28.9	18.8	20.2	28.3	74.6
IADL or other care:					
Meal preparation:**					
No help from network	15.6	32.4	5.1	6.9	1.2
Help from one caregiver	55.3	42.7	74.9	65.4	38.5
Help from more than one caregiver	29.1	24.8	20.0	27.7	60.3
Housework, laundry, shopping, chores:**					
No help from network	2.5	4.3	1.6	1.8	0.4
Help from one caregiver	53.8	52.3	67.4	63.1	15.9
Help from more than one caregiver	43.7	43.4	30.9	35.2	83.7
Managing money:**					
No help from network	18.9	30.7	6.3	16.1	11.5
Help from one caregiver	69.4	57.9	86.5	75.0	62.7
Help from more than one caregiver	11.6	11.4	7.2	8.8	25.8
Any IADL or other care:					
No help from network	0.8	1.6	0.2	0.4	0
Help from one caregiver	49.4	49.0	64.4	57.6	8.3
Help from more than one caregiver	49.8	49.4	35.4	42.0	91.7
Supervision for personal safety:**					
No help from network	57.4	85.2	43.3	41.4	31.0
Help from one caregiver	21.6	7.7	40.2	33.4	7.1
Help from more than one caregiver	21.0	7.1	16.5	25.2	61.9
Any in-home care:					
No help from network	0.5	1.1	0.0	0.2	0.0
Help from one caregiver	46.8	47.5	61.9	54.0	4.4
Help from more than one caregiver	52.7	51.4	38.1	45.8	95.6

Table 5–6 continued

		Caregiving Networks with:			
Type of Care	All Networks	No Live-in Caregiver	One Live-in Caregiver, Spouse	One Live-in Caregiver, Other Than Spouse	More Than One Live-in Caregiver
Services produced outside the home					
Transportation:**					
No help from network	43.7	37.8	53.0	45.6	41.3
Help from one caregiver	39.2	42.5	39.1	41.1	26.2
Help from more than one caregiver	17.1	19.8	7.9	13.4	32.5
Socializing (keeping company)					
No help from network	13.1	16.8	12.3	11.4	6.8
Help from one caregiver	42.2	39.4	57.4	49.1	10.7
Help from more than one caregiver	44.7	43.8	30.2	39.5	82.5

Note on statistical significance: Significance tests were based on the chi-square statistic for cross-tabulations. Significant differences among the distributions in columns 2 through 5 are denoted by asterisks at the relevant type of care: ** denotes statistical significance at the 99 percent level.

money management; as noted above, only one person usually provided help with this task.

The total time devoted by caregiving networks, including the time spent socializing with the care recipient, averaged 6.9 hours per day (see table 5–7)—an average that varied significantly by the composition of the caregiving network. Larger networks provided more hours of care, as did networks in which the care recipient's spouse was a member. Networks which contained at least one live-in caregiver generally devoted three times as many hours to providing care and socializing as did those in which no caregiver lived with the elderly care recipient. It should be noted that because primary caregivers reported that they devoted an average of 5.7 hours per day to their own caregiving activities they are in fact the major source of informal assistance, even in multi-person networks.

Summary

As in other studies, most frail elderly persons in the channeling study received care from one or more informal caregivers—family members,

Table 5–7
**Average Time Devoted to Care Recipient, Including
Socialization, by Network Characteristics**
(hours per day)

Network Characteristic	Hours per Day
Size:**	
One (primary informal caregiver only)	6.0
Two caregivers	6.7
Three to five caregivers	8.2
Caregiving networks with:**	
Spouse only	9.2
Spouse and child(ren)[a]	9.5
Spouse, children, and others	10.1
Spouse and others	8.4
Child(ren) only	6.6
Child(ren) and others	7.7
Others only	4.4
Caregiving networks with:**	
No live-in caregiver	3.3
One live-in caregiver, spouse of care recipient	9.0
One live-in caregiver, other than spouse	8.6
More than one live-in caregiver	10.9
All networks	6.9

Note on statistical significance: Significance tests were based on the F-statistic for analysis of variance: ** denotes statistically significant differences among the groups in the relevant variable at the 99 percent level.
[a]Including children by marriage.

friends, or neighbors. Approximately 60 percent of the elderly who had at least one caregiver also received care from others. This figure points to a somewhat higher prevalence of single-caregiver networks than was reported by Horowitz and Dobrof (1982, 218). Even by restricting their definition of caregiver only to relatives, they concluded that 75 percent of the caregiving networks contained more than one caregiver.

The composition of the caregiving networks in the channeling study was quite diverse. As was expected based on the results of other research, spouses and children played substantial roles in informal caregiving, but other relatives and nonrelatives also provided some care to the elderly care recipient in about half of all caregiving networks. However, networks which consisted solely of nonrelatives and relatives other than spouses and children generally provided less care than did networks in which the spouse and/or child of the care recipient was a member. Also consistent with previous research, networks which contained at least one live-in caregiver generally provided more types of care and more hours of care than did networks which did not contain live-in caregivers.

Almost 60 percent of the elderly in the channeling study had a live-in caregiver.

The larger the caregiver network, the more likely it was to provide each particular type of care and to contain more than one person who shared responsibility for providing that care. However, some types of responsibilities (money management, in particular) were generally not shared, even when the network did contain others. And a division of labor appeared to exist within families—when the spouse of the elderly care recipient was a caregiver, she (or sometimes he) provided the bulk of the day-to-day care tasks, while others helped with household chores and with supervision for personal safety and socializing. Overall, however, the majority of care was provided by a single person—the primary caregiver.

Before we turn to the impact of caregiving on the lives of primary caregivers, we will examine another form of informal support—financial contributions to caring for the elderly person, in the form of paying bills, making cash contributions, and providing gifts of food, clothing, or other items.

Notes

1. Since the interviews did not ascertain the age of caregivers other than the primary caregiver, the "generation" of these other caregivers vis-à-vis the care recipient could not be defined in more precise terms.

2. Some primary caregivers found it difficult to provide even these global time estimates; from 6.6 to 7.5 percent of the primary caregivers reported that they did not know the total amount of time which specific other caregivers devoted to providing care. For this reason, time estimates for the total network (constructed by summing the estimates for all network members) are available only for 1,722 of the 1,940 caregiving networks. Even when answers were provided, it should be remembered that they still represent the estimates of the primary caregiver.

6
Informal Financial Assistance

Financial assistance has not received as much research attention as have other forms of informal support to the elderly, and, in general, the literature suggests that the provision of financial support does not constitute a major activity of informal caregivers. In the General Accounting Office (1977, 19) study conducted in Cleveland, 12 percent of the elderly respondents received financial contributions for housing, 7 percent received contributions for groceries and food, and only 2 percent received contributions for general purposes. However, because the Cleveland sample was chosen randomly from elderly persons who were residing in the community (and, hence, who were not necessarily impaired), these estimates probably underestimate the financial contributions made to the impaired elderly.

Horowitz and Dobrof (1982, 173) documented the financial support provided by primary informal caregivers (defined as including relatives only) to a sample of impaired elderly who were residing in New York City. They found that expenditures for food, clothing, and household items represented the most frequently provided forms of financial assistance; 43.5 percent of the caregivers who were children of the care recipient and 17 percent of other relatives made such contributions. More recently, Caro and Blank (1984, 6) reported that only 36 percent of the primary informal caregivers in their research sample of impaired elderly, also in New York City, made cash expenditures on behalf of the care recipient in the three months prior to their interview.

Relative to previous studies, the channeling study provides an opportunity to examine in greater detail the types and amounts of financial assistance provided through informal financial assistance networks and to add significantly to our knowledge about this aspect of caregiving.

Financial contributions were defined in a very specific way in the channeling study—as regular contributions (that is, made at least once a month) which entailed financial costs because of the elderly person's illness or disability and which were not paid back or reimbursed through insurance. Primary caregivers were asked to provide information on the informal financial assistance provided by others, in much the same way as they reported on the care provided by other members of the informal caregiving network. Thus, because of this approach, elderly persons who may have received financial assistance from friends or relatives, but who had no informal source of personal or household caregiving, are not included in this discussion because no caregivers were available to provide information on financial assistance. In addition, primary caregivers who were the spouses of the care recipients were not asked about any financial assistance that they themselves provided.[1] However, all primary caregivers, regardless of their relationship to the elderly care recipient, were asked to name other relatives or friends who had made financial contributions. These persons could of course have been mentioned previously as a member of the caregiving network, or they could have been persons who provided only financial assistance.

Financial Assistance Networks

Only 37 percent of the elderly in the channeling study were reported to have received any informal financial assistance from someone other than a spouse; moreover, where financial assistance networks existed, they generally consisted only of one person (see table 6–1). Thus, financial

Table 6–1
Characteristics of the Financial Assistance Network
(percent)

Network Characteristic	Percent
Size of financial assistance network:	
None	
Primary caregiver spouse of care recipient	22.0
Primary caregiver not spouse	41.0
One person	32.1
Two persons	3.1
Three to five persons	1.9
Financial assistance network living arrangements:	
None	
Primary caregiver spouse of care recipient	22.0
Primary caregiver not spouse	41.0
At least one live-in financial contributor	17.7
No live-in financial contributor	19.3

Note: Primary caregivers who were spouses were assumed to share all expenses jointly with the care recipient, and, because of the difficulty they were expected to have in identifying those expenses due specifically to the elderly person's illness or disability, spouses were not included in the definition of financial assistance networks.

assistance networks were generally smaller than caregiver networks (see chapter 5). In about half of the cases in which one or more financial contributors were present, at least one lived with the elderly sample member.

The average dollar value of contributions received by elderly sample members from their financial assistance networks was $76 per month (see table 6–2);[2] the average includes zero values for care recipients who had no financial assistance network, including those in which the primary caregiver was the care recipient's spouse and in which no others were available to provide financial assistance. Where financial assistance networks did exist—that is, when elderly care recipients were reported to receive some informal financial assistance from someone other than a spouse and the dollar values of these contributions were provided (a total of 662 cases)—the total financial contribution of the network to the elderly sample member averaged $216 per month. Larger financial assistance networks tended to make larger total contributions, and networks with at least one live-in contributor had higher average expenditures. Elderly care recipients who had low monthly incomes were

Table 6–2
Average Monthly Network Expenditures, by Financial Assistance Network Size and Living Arrangement
(dollars per month)

Network Characteristic	Dollars
Size of financial assistance network:**	
None	
Primary caregiver spouse of care recipient	N.A.
Primary caregiver not spouse	0
One person	181.2
Two persons	263.7
Three to five persons	717.5
Financial assistance network living arrangements:**	
None	
Primary caregiver spouse of care recipient	N.A.
Primary caregiver not spouse	0
At least one live-in financial contributor	272.0
No live-in financial contributor	165.8
All elderly care recipients	76.1

Note: Primary caregivers who were spouses were assumed to share all expenses jointly with the care recipient, and, because of the difficulty they were expected to have in identifying those expenses due specifically to the elderly person's illness or disability, spouses were not included in the definition of financial assistance networks.

Note on statistical significance: Significance tests were based on the F-statistic for analysis of variance: ** denotes statistically significant differences among the groups in the relevant variable at the 99 percent level.

N.A. = Not applicable.

reported to have received significantly more assistance from informal sources (see table 6–3). However, no statistically significant differences in financial assistance network expenditures by insurance coverage were found.

Primary Caregivers Who Provided Financial Assistance

Over 45 percent of the primary caregivers other than the spouses of the elderly provided some financial assistance. This percentage is very similar to the proportion found in the Horowitz and Dobrof study (1982, 182), but is approximately 10 percent greater than the proportion found in the Caro and Blank study (1984, 6). Compared with all nonspouse caregivers, those who made financial contributions were more likely to be living with the care recipient, to be the care recipient's child, to have attended or completed college, to be employed, and to have higher incomes than those who did not provide financial assistance (see table 6–4). In other words, they had closer relationships with the care recipient and a greater capacity to provide financial help than did other caregivers.

Primary caregivers were asked about financial contributions in a number of specific areas:

Cash contributions (providing spending money but not for specific bills)

Table 6–3
Average Monthly Network Expenditures, by Care Recipient Income and Insurance Coverage

Characteristic of Care Recipient	Dollars
Care recipient monthly income:**	
Less than $300	128.0
$300 to $499	96.8
$500 to $999	50.4
$1,000 or more	24.2
Care recipient insurance coverage:	
Medicaid	70.4
Medicare, no Medicaid	77.3
Neither	96.2
All elderly care recipients	76.1

Note: Primary caregivers who were spouses were assumed to share all expenses jointly with the care recipient, and, because of the difficulty they were expected to have in identifying those expenses due specifically to the elderly person's illness or disability, spouses were not included in the definition of financial assistance networks.

Note on statistical significance: Significance tests were based on the F-statistic for analysis of variance: ** denotes statistically significant differences among the groups in the relevant variable at the 99 percent level.

Table 6–4
Sociodemographic Characteristics of All Nonspouse Primary Caregivers and Those Providing Financial Assistance
(percent)

Characteristic of Nonspouse Primary Caregiver	All Nonspouse Primary Caregivers	Nonspouse Caregivers Providing Financial Assistance[a]
Female	76.8	76.2
Gender of caregiver and care recipient:		
Both female	62.6	61.8
Both male	5.6	5.1
Caregiver female, care recipient male	14.1	14.4
Caregiver male, care recipient female	17.6	18.6
Age:		
40 years or younger	15.7	14.0
41 to 54 years	30.0	31.8
55 to 64 years	28.9	32.2
65 to 75 years	19.5	17.6
Older than 75 years	6.0	4.3
Ethnic background:		
Black	24.6	25.2
Hispanic	3.7	4.1
White or other[b]	71.7	70.7
Education completed:		
No formal education	0.2	0
Elementary education	16.5	12.7
Some high school	15.7	14.9
High school	35.1	33.4
Some post–high school	17.6	20.5
College	8.0	9.9
Post-college	6.9	8.7
Caregiver living arrangements vis-à-vis care recipient:		
Lives with care recipient		
Spouse	N.A.	N.A.
Nonspouse	43.8	49.8
Does not live with care recipient	56.2	50.2
Marital status:		
Spouse of care recipient	N.A.	N.A.
Currently married, but not spouse of care recipient	51.0	54.4
Not currently married	49.0	45.6
Any children under age 15	19.7	18.9
Relationship to care recipient:		
Spouse	N.A.	N.A.
Daughter	40.3	47.1
Son	14.3	17.0
Daughter-in-law	5.7	6.2
Sibling or sibling-in-law	9.5	8.7
Other[c]	30.2	21.0
Other caregiving responsibilities:		
Caregiver has other long-term caregiving responsibilities	20.1	22.4
Caregiver does not have other long-term caregiving responsibilities	79.8	77.6

Table 6–4 continued

Characteristic of Nonspouse Primary Caregiver	All Nonspouse Primary Caregivers	Nonspouse Caregivers Providing Financial Assistance[a]
Monthly family income:[d]		
Less than $500	20.0	14.2
$500 to $999	19.6	19.8
$1,000 or more	60.4	66.0
Employment status:		
Currently employed	42.8	48.6
Employed within past year but not currently employed	8.5	8.1
Not currently employed, and not employed within past year	48.7	43.3
Currently employed caregivers[e]		
Hours worked per week:		
Part time (less than 35 hours per week)	29.0	25.7
Full time (35 hours per week or more)	71.0	74.3
Monthly earnings:[f]		
Less than $500	19.7	16.7
$500 to $999	22.8	24.2
$1,000 or more	57.4	59.1
Family income from caregiver earnings:		
25.0 percent or less	9.6	8.6
25.1 to 50.0 percent	18.2	14.7
50.1 to 75.0 percent	23.5	22.3
75.1 percent or more	48.7	54.4

Note: Primary caregivers who were spouses were assumed to share all expenses jointly with the care recipient, and, because of the difficulty they were expected to have in identifying those expenses due specifically to the elderly person's illness or disability, spouses were not included in the definition of financial assistance networks.

N.A. = Not applicable.

[a]There were 1,494 nonspouse caregivers and 681 nonspouse caregivers who provided financial assistance.

[b]Other includes native Americans, Alaskan natives, Asians, or Pacific Islanders (totaling less than 1 percent of the sample).

[c]Other includes parents, sons-in-law, grandchildren, other relatives, friends or neighbors, and employees or volunteers who were friends of the care recipient prior to their providing care.

[d]Family income was asked for the month prior to the interview month. Respondents were asked to report total family income, before taxes and other deductions, in categories. The midpoint of each category was then assigned, and missing data cases were assigned the mean of the reported values.

[e]There were 639 nonspouse caregivers who were employed at the time of their interview and 330 employed nonspouse caregivers who provided financial assistance.

[f]Respondents were asked to report usual monthly earnings, before taxes and other deductions, in actual dollars. If unwilling or unable to provide actual dollar earnings, they were asked to report earnings in categories. Reports in categories were recoded to the mean value of actual dollar reports falling within those categories. Missing data were assigned the overall mean.

Payment of living expenses, including expenses for the purchase of food or clothing, the payment of housing costs (rent or mortgage, utilities, heat, and maintenance), and the provision of other miscellaneous items (such as carfare or cigarettes)

Payment of other bills, including the payment of medical expenses (medical or nursing-home bills, prescription medicines, and special equipment) and of home-care expenses (such as home health aides, visiting nurses, therapists, and home-delivered meals)

The purchase of food or clothing was the most frequently mentioned form of financial assistance, followed by the payment of medical bills, housing costs, and miscellaneous living expenses (see table 6–5). Cash contributions for spending money was the least frequently mentioned category. This latter finding contrasts with the Horowitz and Dobrof (1982, 174) finding that (for their less disabled sample) general cash contributions represented a more likely form of assistance than did expenditures for the purchase of medical care.

As table 6–5 shows, the categories in which the highest average monthly dollar expenditures were reported by primary caregivers were the payments of medical bills, home services, housing, and food or clothing—each averaging about $20 per month among all nonspouse caregivers. Total expenditures averaged almost $84 per month across all categories. Primary caregivers who provided any financial assistance spent an average of over $190 per month. This level of expenditure is consistent with the expenditure levels cited in both the Horowitz and Dobrof (1982, 173) and the Caro and Blank (1985, 328) studies. Approximately three-quarters of the caregivers who provided financial assistance to the elderly in the channeling study contributed more than one-tenth of their total income toward such assistance; approximately one-third of the caregivers who also made financial contributions provided one-fifth or more of their total income.

Although relatively few caregivers reported providing assistance in any particular category (from a low of 77 caregivers who made cash contributions to a high of 403 who paid for food or clothing, of the total of 681 nonspouse caregivers who provided any financial assistance), the monthly expenditures of those who did provide any assistance were quite high, as shown in table 6–5. Caregivers who paid for home health care contributed an average of approximately $276 per month to such care; those who paid for housing contributed $151 per month, and those who paid for medical bills contributed approximately $127 per month. Even cash contributions and other living expenses averaged close to $50 per month for caregivers who made contributions in those categories.

Unlike the contributions made by the *total* financial assistance net-

Table 6–5
Financial Assistance Provided by Nonspouse Primary Caregivers

Category of Expenditure	All Nonspouse Primary Caregivers[a]		Nonspouse Caregivers Providing Any Financial Assistance[b]		Nonspouse Primary Caregivers Providing Financial Assistance in Particular Category	
	Percent Providing Assistance	Dollars per Month	Percent Providing Assistance	Dollars per Month	Dollars per Month	(Sample Size)
Cash contributions (spending money)	5.4	2.5	11.9	5.5	48.1	(77)
Payment of living expenses:						
Food or clothing	28.8	17.1	63.4	38.4	62.2	(403)
Housing, including rent, mortgage payments, utilities, maintenance	12.6	17.9	27.8	39.9	151.1	(176)
Other	11.2	5.8	24.7	12.8	53.9	(159)
Payment of other bills:						
Medical bills, nursing-home bills, prescription medicine, equipment	20.0	24.4	44.0	54.2	126.8	(285)
Care or services, including home health aide, home-delivered meals	7.6	20.0	16.6	44.2	276.4	(108)
Any financial support	45.4	—	100.0	—	—	—
Total expenditures	—	83.7	—	190.8	—	—

[a]Coded as zero if caregiver did not make any financial contributions. There were 1,499 nonspouse caregivers in all.

[b]Includes all nonspouse caregivers who made any financial contribution. If such a caregiver did not provide financial support in a given category, it was coded as zero. There were 681 nonspouse caregivers who provided financial assistance.

work, the contributions made by primary caregivers were not generally greater for care recipients with lower incomes (see table 6–6). This finding suggests that when the elderly care recipient had very limited financial resources the primary caregivers were more likely to help financially, but their contributions were usually supplemented by those made by a larger informal assistance network.

The decision by nonspouse caregivers to provide financial assistance and the amount of such assistance varied by the relationship between and the living arrangements of the caregiver and the recipient. This was true both for total expenditures and for the major expenditure categories (medical bills, home health care, housing costs, and food or clothing). In these categories, children were more likely than other caregivers to provide financial assistance (see table 6–7). Sons were particularly likely to contribute large amounts, averaging almost $135 per month, compared with $106 per month contributed by daughters. This finding suggests that sons may substitute financial assistance for hands-on care.

Differences among caregivers in financial assistance also appeared by living arrangements (see table 6–8). Live-in caregivers were more likely to provide financial assistance, although certain types of expenses (such as miscellaneous living expenses and cash contributions) were more often incurred by caregivers who did not live with the elderly person. Live-in caregivers were more likely to pay for large expense items (such as housing costs and medical expenses), and, overall, they contributed twice the average amount reported by caregivers who did not live with the elderly care recipient—an average of more than $120 per month.

Summary

Financial assistance to the impaired elderly is not as prevalent as hands-on care (a finding which is consistent with other studies). Yet this does not mean that it is provided infrequently. Almost 40 percent of the elderly care recipients in the channeling study received some financial contributions from informal sources, and approximately 45 percent of the primary caregivers other than spouses made such contributions.

When provided, financial assistance was not trivial, averaging $190 among caregivers who contributed cash or in-kind support. Moreover, such assistance was the responsibility of one person more often than was hands-on caregiving. Most informal providers of financial assistance were the only person to do so; only one in twenty shared responsibility with another person for making financial contributions to the care of the elderly person. In addition, those who made such contributions were often those who also provided substantial hands-on help, especially live-

Table 6–6
**Financial Assistance Provided by Nonspouse Primary Caregivers, by Care
Recipient Income**

| | Care Recipient Monthly Income | | | |
| | All Nonspouse Caregivers[a] | | Under $300 | |
Category of Expenditure	Percent Providing Assistance	Dollars per Month	Percent Providing Assistance	Dollars per Month
Cash contributions (spending money)	5.4*	2.5	9.8	3.6
Payment of living expenses:				
Food or clothing	28.8	17.1*	34.0	23.7
Housing, including rent, mortgage payments, utilities, maintenance	12.6	17.9	16.4	17.0
Other	11.2	5.8	11.1	5.8
Payment of other bills:				
Medical bills, nursing-home bills, prescription medicine, and equipment	20.0*	24.4	25.1	29.8
Care or services, including home health aide, home-delivered meals	7.6	20.0	8.6	32.0
Any financial support	45.4**	—	51.6	—
Total expenditures	—	83.7	—	112.9

Note on statistical significance: Significance tests for the percent providing assistance were based on the chi-square statistic for cross-tabulations. Significance tests for dollars per month were based on the F-statistic for analysis of variance. Significant differences in the distributions between columns are denoted by asterisk(s) at the entry for the relevant variable in the first columns: * denotes statistical significance at the 95 percent level; ** denotes statistical significance at the 99 percent level.

[a]Coded as zero if caregiver did not provide financial support in given category.

in caregivers. Conversely, the large contributions of sons, who generally do not provide much hands-on care, may represent another aspect of the sexual division of labor in caregiving.

Notes

1. This decision was based on the presumption that spouses would find it difficult to disaggregate regularly shared expenses. Because of this restriction, total network expenditures for care recipients with spouses (who are likely to have incurred expenditures associated with caregiving) are understated.

| | Care Recipient Monthly Income | | | | |
| $300 to $499 | | $500 to $999 | | $1,000 and Over | |
Percent Providing Assistance	Dollars per Month	Percent Providing Assistance	Dollars per Month	Percent Providing Assistance	Dollars per Month
4.5	1.7	4.7	3.0	4.0	3.0
28.6	15.6	27.0	16.1	23.7	15.1
12.3	19.1	11.7	15.9	9.2	21.8
11.7	5.8	10.6	5.9	10.5	3.8
20.9	27.9	17.1	27.9	12.8	9.8
7.8	21.6	6.8	21.6	6.6	5.9
47.2	—	41.0	—	34.2	—
—	83.3	—	72.3	—	58.5

2. If primary caregivers could not provide specific dollar amounts contributed either by themselves or by others, the interviewer asked about possible ranges. Responses that were recorded in ranges were recoded into dollar amounts by assigning the midpoint of the range (for example, if a caregiver reported expenses in the $100 to $300 range, $200 was assigned). The open-ended ranges at the two extremes were treated differently: if the caregiver's response was in the range "$100 or less," the average dollar amount for caregivers who had reported exact dollar expenditures of up to and including $100 was computed and assigned. A similar procedure was used to compute expenditures at the upper end of the expenditure range. Therefore, the expenditure figures presented in this report should be interpreted as general indications of the magnitude of such contributions rather than as precise estimates.

Table 6–7
Expenditures by Nonspouse Primary Caregiver, by Relationship to Care Recipient

Category of Expenditure	All Nonspouse Caregivers[a]		Daughter	
	Percent Providing Assistance	Dollars per Month	Percent Providing Assistance	Dollars per Month
Cash contributions (spending money)	5.4	22.5	4.8	1.9
Payment of living expenses:				
Food or clothing**	28.8**	17.1**	35.1	21.2
Housing, including rent, mortgage payments, utilities, maintenance	12.6**	17.9**	15.4	24.0
Other	11.2	5.8	11.9	5.2
Payment of other bills:				
Medical bills, nursing-home bills, prescription medicine, and equipment	20.0**	24.4*	25.7	33.7
Care or services, including home health aide, home-delivered meals	7.6**	20.0**	9.1	28.3
Any financial support	45.4**	—	53.2	—
Total expenditures	—	83.7**	—	106.2

Note on statistical significance: Significance tests for the percent providing assistance were based on the chi-square statistics for cross-tabulations. Significance tests for dollars per month were based on the F-statistic for analysis of variance. Significant differences among entries in columns 2 through 6 are denoted by asterisk(s) at the entry for the relevant variable in the first columns: * denotes statistical significance at the 95 percent level; ** denotes statistical significance at the 99 percent level.

[a]Coded as zero if caregiver did not provide financial support in given category.
[b]Includes siblings-in-law.

Relationship to Care Recipient							
Son		Daughter-in-Law		Sibling[b]		Other	
Percent Providing Assistance	*Dollars per Month*	*Percent Providing Assistance*	*Dollars per Month*	*Percent Providing Assistance*	*Dollars per Month*	*Percent Providing Assistance*	*Dollars per Month*
8.4	5.8	5.8	2.0	5.0	3.2	4.9	1.6
33.2	23.7	33.7	24.8	27.0	12.9	17.9	8.5
20.7	24.8	15.1	19.1	7.1	16.8	6.4	6.9
11.2	7.6	9.3	6.1	10.6	5.9	10.8	5.5
27.0	30.1	17.6	28.4	17.7	16.5	10.2	11.0
15.4	42.8	12.8	9.3	3.6	12.4	2.0	2.6
54.0	—	48.8	—	41.6	—	31.6	—
—	134.8	—	88.2	—	64.6	—	35.6

Table 6–8
Expenditures by Nonspouse Primary Caregiver, by Living Arrangement

Category of Expenditure	All Nonspouse Primary Caregivers[a]		Nonspouse Caregivers Living with Care Recipient		Nonspouse Caregivers Not Living with Care Recipient	
	Percent Providing Assistance	Dollars per Month	Percent Providing Assistance	Dollars per Month	Percent Providing Assistance	Dollars per Month
Cash contributions (spending money)	5.4	2.5	4.7	2.4	5.9	2.5
Payment of living expenses:						
Food or clothing	28.8*	17.1**	32.7	23.0	25.7	12.5
Housing, including rent, mortgage payments, utilities, maintenance	12.6**	17.9**	20.1	26.6	6.9	11.4
Other	11.2*	5.8	8.9	6.3	13.0	5.3
Payment of other bills:						
Medical bills, nursing-home bills, prescription medicine, and equipment	20.0**	24.4**	28.5	41.3	13.4	11.4
Care or services, including home health aide, home-delivered meals	7.6**	20.0*	10.0	28.9	5.7	13.1
Any financial support	45.4**	—	51.7	—	40.6	—
Total expenditures	—	83.7**	—	121.5	—	54.7

Note on statistical significance: Significance tests for the percent providing assistance were based on the chi-square statistic for cross-tabulations. Significance tests for dollars per month were based on the F-statistic for analysis of variance. Significant differences between entries in columns 2 and 3 are denoted by asterisk(s) at the entry for the relevant variable in the first columns; * denotes statistical significance at the 95 percent level; ** denotes statistical significance at the 99 percent level.
[a]Coded as zero if caregiver did not provide financial support in given category.

7
The Well-Being of Caregivers

T he common observation in the extensive literature on the well-being of persons who provide care to the elderly is that caregiving is stressful; the greater the burdens placed on the caregiver by caregiving and the caregiving situation, the more the well-being of caregivers is likely to suffer, and the less able they will be to continue to provide care. Caregiving clearly imposes limitations on alternate activities in which the caregiver might choose to engage, whether these activities constitute employment, leisure-time pursuits, or ongoing relationships with other family members. Other aspects of the caregiving situation, such as the quality of the relationship between the caregiver and the care recipient and the behavioral problems of the care recipient, can also add to the burden of caregiving. This chapter examines a number of measures pertaining to the well-being of caregivers and explores the interrelationships among them.

Before doing so, however, it is important to point out the limitations imposed on our analysis by the cross-sectional nature of the data. Caregiving and the well-being of caregivers were measured simultaneously in the caregiver survey results reported herein. Since the effect of caregiving on well-being is likely to be cumulative and, in some cases, reciprocal (for example, caregivers who experience physical strain because of the ongoing demands of caregiving may become incapacitated themselves and be forced to reduce their caregiving efforts), measures of caregiving and the well-being of caregivers obtained at the same time are not strictly appropriate for drawing inferences about cause and effect—even though most measures of well-being in this study are based on survey questions which place the response directly within the context of providing care to the care recipient.[1] For this reason, we examine the relationships among measures of caregiving and the well-being of caregivers, but avoid making statements about the effects of caregiving on well-being.

Restrictions Imposed by Caregiving

Past studies have pointed out the restrictions imposed on caregivers by providing care to an elderly person. A major source of stress is the constraint on personal freedom which often accompanies a commitment to informal caregiving (Caro and Blank 1984). In case studies of the relationships between children and their elderly parents, Robinson and Thurnher (1979, 591) discovered that the actual activities of providing care were perceived to be less burdensome than the restrictions on personal freedom imposed by the caregiving routine. For instance, as a result of the daily demands of caregiving, several of their respondents had not taken a vacation for years. This aspect of caregiving was especially resented by children at the age of retirement, who felt deprived of the opportunity to enjoy their retirement freedom.

In the channeling study, primary informal caregivers were presented with several possible ways in which providing care to the care recipient might impose constraints on their personal life:

1. Limiting the time available to spend with children or other family members
2. Limiting personal privacy
3. Limiting social life or free time
4. Requiring that the caregiver pay constant attention to the care recipient
5. Creating difficulties with other close relationships

Primary caregivers were asked to indicate whether each aspect of caregiving posed a problem and, if a problem, whether or not they considered it serious. Each type of personal restriction was then coded as (1) a serious problem, (2) a problem which was not perceived to be serious, or (3) not a problem at all.

For each type of potential limitation, at least one-third of the primary informal caregivers in the channeling study reported some degree of restriction, and for some types the proportions who reported restrictions due to caregiving were much higher (see table 7–1). For example, although almost 65 percent reported experiencing no problems with caregiving vis-à-vis other relationships and although 59 percent stated that they experienced no loss of privacy due to caregiving, more than half of the primary caregivers reported problems in terms of the time available to them to spend with their families and in terms of the necessity of providing constant attention to the needs of the elderly person as part of the responsibilities of caregiving. And approximately two-thirds of all

Table 7–1
**Personal Limitations Imposed by Caregiving, Reported by
Primary Caregiver**

Limitation	Percent
Limits on time with family:	
Serious problem	23.8
A problem, but not serious	29.8
Not a problem	46.3
Restricted privacy due to caregiving:	
Serious problem	16.8
A problem, but not serious	24.3
Not a problem	58.8
Limits on social life due to caregiving:	
Serious problem	31.9
A problem, but not serious	34.9
Not a problem	33.2
Caregiving requires constant attention:	
Serious problem	29.0
A problem, but not serious	24.0
Not a problem	47.0
Caregiving hard on other relationships:	
Serious problem	22.4
A problem, but not serious	13.0
Not a problem	64.6

caregivers reported experiencing restrictions in their social lives due to their caregiving activities. Overall, more than three-quarters reported that caregiving imposed at least one restriction on their personal lives.

Other sources of stress associated with informal caregiving seem to pertain to role conflicts. Horowitz (1978, 7) noted that these role conflicts usually center around the competing demands of caring for one's spouse and children and of caring for one's parents. By its nature, setting priorities among these demands involves tremendous emotional conflict, conflict which is not resolved at the point at which choices are made. These choices usually involve the division of either the time or the income devoted to the parent and the spouse and/or children. With respect to female children who act as caregivers, more women are being forced to choose between helping their frail parents and bringing in the income necessary to support themselves and their families (Treas 1977, 489; Brody 1979). The number of these types of conflicts is likely to increase in the future as the declining number of children coincides with an increase both in the life expectancy of the aged parent and the opportunities available for females to participate in the labor force. Between 1940 and 1978, the proportion of married women between the ages of 45 and 54 in the labor force increased from 11 percent to almost 53 percent, and even higher rates were observed for single, separated, divorced, and widowed women at those ages (Brody 1979, 1832). In a recently completed study, Brody (1985, 25) found that 28 percent of a sample of nonworking women had quit their jobs because of the demands of providing informal care to their mothers.

Restrictions on the employment of the primary caregivers in the channeling demonstration were examined separately for three categories of caregivers: those who were employed at the time of the interview, those who were not then employed but who had been employed within the year prior to the interview, and those who had not been employed in the year prior to the interview but who were under age 70. Caregivers who were 70 years of age or older and who were not employed were assumed no longer to be in the active labor force and, hence, were not asked questions about restrictions on employment.[2]

Caregivers were asked whether their caregiving responsibilities had imposed any of four possible employment-related restrictions on them within the year prior to the interview:

1. Whether they worked fewer hours than they desired
2. Whether they were forced to quit a job
3. Whether they were forced to turn down a job or to refuse a more responsible position
4. Whether they were unable to search for a job (or another job) when they wanted employment

Caregivers who were not recently or currently employed were asked only the last two questions.

Caregivers in all three groups reported employment-related restrictions due to caregiving (see table 7–2). Almost one-third of both currently and recently employed caregivers had experienced restricted working hours. Over 35 percent of the unemployed caregivers who had recently worked had left jobs in the past year in order to provide care, over 21 percent had turned down a job, and over 28 percent had been unable to search for work due to their caregiving responsibilities. Among the currently employed caregivers, approximately 9 to 12 percent had experienced some negative effects of caregiving on their ability to seek or retain suitable employment or to take advantage of job-advancement opportunities. Even caregivers who were not recently in the labor market felt restricted in their desired employment opportunities: almost 18 percent stated that they were unable to search for work, and almost 8 percent stated that caregiving responsibilities had forced them to decline an employment opportunity.

Table 7–2
Employment Limitations Imposed by Caregiving, Reported by Primary Caregiver

Limitation	Percent
Currently employed caregivers[a]	
Working hours:	
Restricted due to caregiving in past year	32.7
Not restricted	67.3
Leaving jobs:	
Had to leave a job in past year	9.0
Did not have to leave a job	91.0
Taking or changing job:	
Had to turn down a job or refuse more responsible position in past year	12.4
Did not have to turn down a job	87.6
Looking for a(nother) job:	
Unable to look for a job in past year	8.6
Able to look for a job	91.4
Recently employed caregivers[b]	
Working hours:	
Restricted due to caregiving in past year	32.5
Not restricted	67.6
Leaving jobs:	
Had to leave a job within past year	35.3
Did not have to leave job	64.7
Taking or changing job:	
Had to turn down a job or refuse more responsible position in past year	21.2
Did not have to turn down a job	78.8
Looking for a(nother) job:	
Unable to look for work in past year	28.5
Able to look for a job	71.5
Caregivers neither currently nor recently employed[c]	
Taking or changing job:	
Had to turn down a job in past year	7.9
Did not have to turn down a job	92.0
Looking for a(nother) job:	
Unable to look for work in past year	17.6
Able to look for a job	82.4

Note: The 496 caregivers who were 70 years of age or older were not asked these questions.

[a]There were 661 caregivers under age 70 who were employed at the time of their interviews.

[b]There were 137 caregivers under age 70 who were not employed at the time of their interviews but who had been employed within the year prior to the interview.

[c]There were 642 caregivers under age 70 who were not employed within the year prior to the interview.

Care Recipient Behavior

The stresses associated with caregiving can be exacerbated if the care recipient's behavior strains the caregiving relationship. The long-term disability or illness of a family member and its related caregiving burdens can seriously strain even the most solid of relationships (Monk 1979). Regardless of the source of stress, Robinson and Thurnher (1979, 591–592) believe that it increases with the passage of time, the physical deterioration of the elderly care recipient, and the additional demands it inevitably places on the informal caregiver.[3]

The primary caregivers in the channeling study were asked about the quality of their interaction with the care recipient. They were also asked to describe several aspects of the elderly person's behavior which could indicate a stressful caregiving situation:

1. Whether the care recipient said or did things that embarrassed the caregiver or others
2. Whether the care recipient sometimes became angry and yelled at the caregiver, or refused to cooperate
3. Whether the care recipient forgot things or became confused, and, if so, whether these conditions represented a serious problem for the caregiver

Primary caregivers generally described their relationship with the elderly care recipients as one in which they were "getting along very well" (see table 7–3); very few reported that they did not get along too well. Relatively few caregivers reported that the behavior of the care recipients could be considered embarrassing. However, almost half of the caregivers had to face either the anger of or the lack of cooperation from care recipients, and 70 percent reported some level of confusion experienced by the care recipient, although only 30 percent felt that the latter presented a serious problem. A large majority (78.3 percent) reported at least one of these three behavioral problems. Given the possible reluctance of caregivers to report the negative characteristics of their elderly relative or friends, the findings suggest that informal caregivers often face difficult circumstances stemming directly from the behavior of the care recipient, in addition to the demands imposed by the caregiving activities themselves.

Care Alternatives and Arrangements

As we discussed in chapter 4, over 40 percent of all primary caregivers reported that they were the only source of informal care for the elderly

Table 7–3
Care Recipient Behavior, Reported by Primary Caregiver

Behavior of Care Recipient	Percentage
Quality of interaction with care recipient:	
Gets along very well	72.0
Gets along fairly well	24.6
Does not get along too well	3.4
Care recipient's behavior is embarrassing:	
Sometimes embarrasses caregiver or others	23.3
Behavior not embarrassing	76.7
Care recipient becomes angry or is uncooperative:	
Sometimes becomes upset and yells at caregiver or refuses to cooperate	49.5
Not angry or uncooperative	50.5
Care recipient is forgetful or confused:	
Sometimes forgets things or gets confused—a serious problem	30.2
Sometimes forgets things or gets confused—not a serious problem	40.6
Not forgetful or confused	29.2

care recipient. Therefore, perceptions of the availability of sources of care, formal or informal, and concern about the effectiveness and coverage of care arrangements are likely to be important aspects of the well-being of caregivers.

To address this issue, the channeling study asked primary caregivers to rate their satisfaction with all arrangements, formal and informal, for providing care for the elderly care recipient. They were also asked to indicate how much they worried about obtaining sufficient help or assistance for their elderly relative or friend. Most caregivers (over 65 percent) were very satisfied or at least somewhat satisfied with their current arrangements for care (see table 7–4). However, more than half worried much of the time, and almost 80 percent worried at least sometimes, about whether sufficient help for the elderly person would be available. This concern over future arrangements, rather than the immediate need for assistance, may well have been the impetus for many to apply for channeling demonstration services on behalf of the care recipient.

A similar pattern is reflected in measures of the availability of care alternatives. Although almost 60 percent of the primary caregivers reported that someone else in the informal caregiving network provided at least some care to the care recipient, less than 30 percent believed that someone else would be available to provide the same care as they did, if they could no longer provide care. However, few believed that the care recipient would have to be placed in a nursing home in the following year, suggesting that many primary caregivers strongly resist the idea of institutionalization, even when they are concerned about the availability of help.

Table 7–4
Caregiver Satisfaction with Care Arrangements and Available Care Alternatives

Opinion of Primary Caregiver	Percentage
Satisfaction with care arrangements	
Caregiver satisfaction with care arrangements:	
Very satisfied	33.2
Somewhat satisfied	32.3
Not too satisfied	20.6
No other arrangements	13.9
Worries about sufficient help for care recipient:	
Quite a lot	50.7
Sometimes	27.8
Rarely	8.2
Not at all	13.2
Available care alternatives	
Availability of others in network:	
Others in caregiving network	59.1
No others in caregiving network	40.9
Availability of respite care, reported by primary caregiver:[a]	
Someone else available to provide same types of care	27.9
No one else available to provide same types of care	72.1
Probability of nursing-home placement within next year:	
Currently in nursing home	2.5
Certainly will be placed in a nursing home	7.9
Probably will	2.5
Even chance	14.2
Probably will not	17.1
Certainly will not	55.4

[a]This question read: "Now, please think about all of *name of elderly person's* friends and family members *and* people who may help (him/her) as part of their paid or volunteer work. If you were unable to help *name of elderly person,* is there someone who would do the things that you do?"

Strain or Stress Experienced by Caregivers

Examining the restrictions and concerns associated with caregiving represents one approach for assessing the well-being of caregivers. Attempts have also been made to measure the effects on the overall emotional state, health, and personal finances of caregivers. Following the latter approach, the channeling study included three summary questions to gauge caregivers' own perceptions of their levels of emotional, physical, and financial strain.[4] For each, primary caregivers were asked to choose a number between one and five that corresponded to the amount of each type of perceived strain imposed on them by caregiving responsibilities. The two extremes of the response scale were "little or no strain" (number one) and "a great deal of strain" (number five). The intermediate numbers were not labeled, but caregivers were told that they could choose any number on the scale.

Primary caregivers generally reported high levels of emotional strain (see table 7–5). They also generally reported more emotional than other types of strain due to caregiving—almost half reported either a 4 or 5 on the emotional-strain scale. Somewhat fewer, but still almost 40 percent, reported levels of physical strain at the highest points on the scale. Conversely, most primary caregivers (almost 60 percent) experienced little or no financial strain associated with caregiving. The high level of emotional strain, in both absolute terms and relative to other types of strain, corresponds to the findings of other studies. In her recent literature review, Brody (1985, 22) noted that emotional stress as a result of caregiving is the type of strain that is most often cited and which has the greatest impact. After reviewing the available literature, Horowitz and Dobrof (1982, 203) also concluded that financially related stress is unimportant relative to the emotional stress associated with caregiving—a conclusion based in part on the work of Cantor (1980).

In the remainder of this section we examine the relationships among the three measures of strain and more objective aspects of caregiving and the characteristics of caregivers.

Emotional Strain

The gender of the caregiver, his or her relationship to the care recipient, and his or her living arrangements were all significantly correlated with reported emotional strain, as were measures of the care provided (see table 7–6). Women who provided care to elderly recipients reported experiencing greater emotional stress than their male counterparts; wives, daughters, and daughters-in-law also experienced greater strain than did

Table 7–5
Emotional, Physical, and Financial Strain, Reported by Primary Caregiver
(percent)

| Type of Strain | Strain Scale | | | | |
	A Great Deal 5	4	3	2	Little or None 1
Emotional strain	37.0	12.7	22.2	10.3	17.8
Physical strain	26.1	12.1	18.2	12.1	32.6
Financial strain	12.7	5.8	13.4	10.8	57.4

Note: Only the two extreme values of the scales were labeled.

Table 7-6
Reported Emotional Strain, by Caregiver Characteristics and Measures of Caregiving
(percent)

Characteristic/Care Provided	Emotional Strain Scale				
	A Great Deal 5	4	3	2	Little or None 1
Caregiver gender:**					
Male	29.1	12.2	22.6	14.0	22.0
Female	39.8	12.9	22.1	8.9	16.2
Relationship to care recipient:**					
Spouse	46.0	11.4	20.8	9.8	11.9
Daughter	45.8	16.0	20.6	8.2	9.5
Son	30.0	16.7	27.1	11.9	14.3
Daughter-in-law	42.4	11.8	24.7	7.1	14.1
Sibling[a]	34.5	12.2	20.9	6.5	25.9
Other	19.4	7.9	23.5	14.7	34.5
Living arrangement:**					
Lives with care recipient:					
Spouse	46.1	11.5	20.6	9.8	11.9
Nonspouse	40.5	12.7	19.8	9.7	17.3
Does not live with care recipient	29.6	13.3	25.0	10.9	21.2
Provision of personal care:**					
Any personal care provided	41.7	13.2	21.1	9.6	14.4
No personal care provided	25.6	11.2	25.1	11.9	26.2
Average hours per day devoted to all care:[b]**					
One hour or less per day	21.8	12.6	25.0	12.6	28.0
1.01 to 2.00 hours per day	30.0	11.2	28.2	12.4	18.2
2.01 to 4.00 hours per day	34.6	20.3	21.2	9.7	14.3
4.01 to 6.00 hours per day	34.0	15.1	23.3	12.9	14.7
6.01 to 8.00 hours per day	38.5	9.5	21.6	9.5	20.8
More than 8 hours per day	46.0	11.4	19.4	10.2	13.0

Note: Only the two extreme values of the scale were labeled.

Note on statistical significance: Significance tests were based on the chi-square statistic for cross-tabulations. Significant differences in the distributions among columns 1 through 5 are denoted by asterisk(s) at the relevant variable: * denotes statistical significance at the 95 percent level; ** denotes statistical significance at the 99 percent level.

[a]Includes siblings-in-law.

[b]Includes time devoted to socializing.

other caregivers, regardless of their gender. The same was true of caregivers who lived with the care recipient. Moreover, the type and level of care provided were also associated with emotional strain. Caregivers who devoted more hours per day to caregiving activities and who provided any type of personal care (assistance in bathing, dressing, eating, getting out of bed or a chair, or toileting) frequently reported high levels of emotional strain.

Regardless of the area of personal restriction (time for oneself or one's family, and the quality of other relationships), caregivers who reported a serious restriction were twice as likely to state that they were under a great deal of emotional strain as were caregivers for whom such limitations did not exist or who perceived them as less serious (see table 7–7). The same basic pattern held for restrictions on employment—

Table 7–7
Reported Emotional Strain, by Limitations Imposed by Caregiving
(percent)

	Emotional Strain Scale				
	A Great Deal				*Little or None*
Limitation	*5*	*4*	*3*	*2*	*1*
Personal limitations					
Limits on time with family:**					
Serious problem	69.0	13.3	13.3	2.2	2.2
A problem, but not serious	31.1	16.6	28.4	10.7	13.1
Not a problem	23.4	10.2	22.6	14.5	29.2
Restricted privacy due to caregiving:**					
Serious problem	68.0	13.3	14.2	2.2	2.2
A problem, but not serious	35.9	15.3	25.0	12.2	11.6
Not a problem	28.2	11.6	23.5	11.8	24.9
Limits on social life due to caregiving:**					
Serious problem	63.7	12.8	16.2	4.5	2.8
A problem, but not serious	27.8	16.0	27.7	12.9	15.5
Not a problem	20.1	9.3	21.9	13.5	35.2
Caregiving requires constant attention:**					
Serious problem	62.2	15.2	15.8	4.0	2.7
A problem, but not serious	33.0	13.9	21.6	12.5	18.9
Not a problem	22.4	10.8	26.5	13.3	27.0

Table 7–7 continued

Limitation	Emotional Strain Scale				
	A Great Deal 5	4	3	2	Little or None 1
Caregiving hard on relationship:**					
Serious problem	69.6	12.5	14.2	1.9	1.9
A problem, but not serious	36.9	18.7	30.7	7.0	6.6
Not a problem	25.2	11.6	23.3	13.9	26.0
Employment-related limitations—currently employed caregivers[a]					
Working hours:**					
Restricted due to caregiving	47.5	18.3	18.8	8.9	6.4
Not restricted	26.0	12.9	26.5	12.2	22.4
Leaving jobs:					
Had to leave a job in past year	36.2	17.2	19.0	6.9	20.7
Did not have to leave a job	32.9	13.9	25.0	11.2	17.0
Taking or changing job:**					
Had to turn down a job or refuse more responsible position in past year	47.6	9.8	29.3	6.1	7.3
Did not have to turn down a job	31.2	14.8	23.9	11.5	18.6
Looking for a(nother) job:**					
Unable to look for a job in past year	56.1	10.5	21.0	5.3	7.0
Able to look for a job	31.0	14.5	24.9	11.4	18.2
Employment-Related Limitations—Recently Employed Caregivers[b]					
Working hours:					
Restricted due to caregiving in past year	44.4	13.9	13.9	13.9	13.9
Not restricted	28.4	10.8	24.3	13.5	23.0
Leaving job:**					
Had to leave a job in past year	56.2	6.2	16.7	8.3	12.5
Did not have to leave job	24.1	11.5	21.8	17.2	25.3
Taking or changing job:					
Had to turn down a job or refuse more responsible position in past year	51.7	3.4	20.7	13.8	10.3

Table 7–7 continued

Limitation	Emotional Strain Scale				
	A Great Deal				Little or None
	5	4	3	2	1
Did not have to turn down a job	30.8	12.2	19.6	14.0	23.4
Looking for a(nother) job:					
Unable to look for work in past year	43.6	7.7	25.6	7.7	15.4
Able to look for a job	32.0	11.3	17.5	16.5	22.7
Employment-Related Limitations—Caregivers neither Currently nor Recently Employed[c]					
Taking or changing job:*					
Had to turn down a job or refuse more responsible position in past year	58.8	13.7	11.8	7.8	7.8
Did not have to turn down a job	38.5	12.6	20.6	10.4	18.0
Looking for a(nother) job:**					
Unable to look for work in past year	53.1	13.3	18.6	8.8	6.2
Able to look for a job	37.2	12.6	20.2	10.5	19.6

Note: Only the two extreme values of the scale were labeled. The 496 caregivers who were 70 years of age or older were not asked the questions on employment.

Note on statistical significance: Significance tests were based on the chi-square statistic for cross-tabulations. Significant differences in the distributions among columns 1 through 5 are denoted by asterisk(s) at the relevant variable: * denotes statistical significance at the 95 percent level; ** denotes statistical significance at the 99 percent level.

[a]There were 661 caregivers under age 70 who were employed at the time of their interviews.

[b]There were 137 caregivers under age 70 who were not employed at the time of their interviews but who had been employed within the year prior to the interview.

[c]There were 642 caregivers under age 70 who were not employed within the year prior to the interview.

caregivers who experienced these limitations reported higher levels of emotional strain—but the relationships were not as strong as they were for restrictions on the personal lives and family relationships of caregivers, nor were they always statistically significant.

The behavioral characteristics of the care recipients as reported by caregivers were also associated with the emotional strain of caregiving. For example, even though relatively few caregivers reported that the care recipient's behavior was embarrassing, that his or her confusion and memory losses did represent a serious problem, or that they did not get along very well with the elderly care recipient, those who did report such problems were especially likely to experience high levels of emotional strain (see table 7–8).

Concern about care arrangements was also significantly associated with emotional strain (see table 7–9). Those caregivers who were dissatisfied with current care arrangements or who worried much of the time about obtaining sufficient help for the care recipient very often reported high levels of emotional strain, as did caregivers who reported

Table 7–8
Reported Emotional Strain, by Care Recipient Behavior
(percent)

Behavior of Care Recipient	Emotional Strain Scale				
	A Great Deal 5	4	3	2	*Little or None* 1
Care recipient becomes angry or is uncooperative:**					
Sometimes becomes upset and yells at caregiver or refuses to cooperate	47.0	13.6	22.4	7.9	9.0
Not angry or uncooperative	27.0	11.8	22.0	12.6	26.5
Care recipient's behavior is embarrassing:**					
Sometimes embarrasses caregiver or others	52.0	12.2	23.1	6.3	6.3
Behavior not embarrassing	32.4	12.9	21.9	11.5	21.4
Care recipient is forgetful or confused:**					
Sometimes forgets things or gets confused—a serious problem	54.5	14.9	20.3	6.1	4.2
Sometimes forgets things or gets confused—not a serious problem	29.4	13.4	23.7	12.7	20.8
Not forgetful or confused	28.5	9.5	22.8	11.3	27.9
Quality of interaction with care recipient:**					
Gets along very well	32.3	11.3	23.0	11.7	21.7
Gets along fairly well	45.3	17.0	21.3	7.4	8.9
Does not get along too well	73.8	12.3	9.2	3.1	1.5

Note: Only the two extreme values of the scale were labeled.

Note on statistical significance: Significance tests were based on the chi-square statistic for cross-tabulations. Significant differences in the distributions among columns 1 through 5 are denoted by asterisk(s) at the relevant variable: * denotes statistical significance at the 95 percent level; ** denotes statistical significance at the 99 percent level.

Table 7–9
Reported Emotional Strain, by Care Alternatives and Other Caregiving Responsibilities
(percent)

	Emotional Strain Scale				
Opinion of Primary Caregiver	*A Great Deal* 5	4	3	2	*Little or None* 1
Satisfaction with care arrangements					
Caregiver satisfaction with care arrangements:**					
Very satisfied	32.6	8.3	21.2	11.7	26.3
Somewhat satisfied	30.7	17.1	25.0	11.1	16.1
Not too satisfied	52.6	10.8	22.4	6.7	7.5
No other arrangements	37.9	16.7	18.6	10.6	16.3
Worries about sufficient help for care recipient:**					
Quite a lot	50.9	14.6	18.9	7.4	8.6
Sometimes	23.9	13.6	29.7	14.2	18.6
Rarely	21.2	6.4	24.4	15.4	32.7
Not at all	19.8	7.3	18.6	9.7	44.5
Available care alternatives					
Availability of others in network:					
Others in caregiving network	35.0	13.4	23.4	10.4	17.9
No others in caregiving network	40.0	11.7	20.6	10.0	17.6
Availability of respite care, reported by primary caregiver:**					
Someone else available to provide same types of care	27.4	9.8	24.9	13.5	24.5
No one else available to provide same types of care	41.2	13.8	21.7	8.9	14.4
Probability of nursing-home placement within next year:**					
Currently in nursing home	48.8	11.6	16.3	4.6	18.6
Certainly will	56.4	12.1	17.1	5.7	8.6
Probably will	34.1	15.9	34.1	11.4	4.6
Even chance	44.9	19.1	19.9	8.2	7.8
Probably will not	36.0	13.3	22.7	11.0	17.0
Certainly will not	31.1	11.0	24.0	11.3	22.5
Other caregiving responsibilities					
Caregiver has other long-term caregiving responsibilities	38.8	15.9	23.4	8.1	13.8

Table 7–9 continued

Opinion of Primary Caregiver	Emotional Strain Scale				
	A Great Deal 5	4	3	2	Little or None 1
Caregiver does not have other long-term caregiving responsibilities	36.7	12.1	22.0	10.8	18.5

Note: Only the two extreme values of the scale were labeled.

Note on statistical significance: Significance tests were based on the chi-square statistic for cross-tabulations. Significant differences in the distributions among columns 1 through 5 are denoted by asterisks at the relevant variable: ** denotes statistical significance at the 99 percent level.

either that no others were available to provide informal support or that no one was available to take over their caregiving tasks. Most caregivers who believed that the elderly person would almost certainly have to be placed in a nursing home within the following year also reported a great deal of emotional strain. However, whether the strain was due to the guilt and anxiety often associated with the decision for nursing-home placement or was due to the fact that the burden of caregiving led the caregiver to consider such placement cannot be determined.

Physical Strain

Reported physical strain was also strongly associated with the characteristics and experiences of caregivers. As was the case with emotional strain, women, live-in caregivers, and, in particular, spouses and daughters reported higher levels of physical strain due to caregiving than did other caregivers (see table 7–10). Caregivers who described their overall health as poor or who reported limitations in their ability to perform personal-care tasks were also especially likely to experience physical strain due to caregiving. Not surprisingly, a strong positive association existed between reports of physical strain and whether personal care was provided and the number of hours of care devoted to all tasks (see table 7–11).

Dissatisfaction with care arrangements and worries about whether sufficient help would be available for the care recipient were also significantly associated with physical strain, probably reflecting the concerns of caregivers who themselves faced health problems and felt that care-

Table 7–10
Reported Physical Strain, by Caregiver Gender, Relationship to Care Recipient, Living Arrangement, and Health
(percent)

Characteristic of Primary Caregiver	Physical Strain Scale				
	A Great Deal 5	4	3	2	Little or None 1
Caregiver gender:**					
Male	17.9	10.0	14.4	14.2	43.5
Female	29.1	11.3	19.5	11.4	28.6
Relationship to care recipient:**					
Spouse	40.0	12.9	17.1	10.2	19.9
Daughter	33.4	13.0	21.0	11.2	21.5
Son	13.9	10.0	13.9	18.7	43.5
Daughter-in-law	18.8	12.9	21.2	12.9	34.1
Sibling[a]	24.3	7.9	18.6	13.6	35.7
Other	10.4	7.5	16.7	11.8	53.6
Living arrangement:**					
Lives with care recipient					
Spouse	40.0	12.7	17.1	10.2	19.9
Nonspouse	31.6	11.1	18.1	11.6	27.6
Does not live with care recipient	14.6	10.0	18.8	13.6	43.0
Self-reported overall health:**					
Excellent	13.7	7.1	15.5	12.9	50.8
Good	18.8	11.0	20.6	14.1	35.5
Fair	32.0	12.1	19.7	12.7	23.5
Poor	55.3	14.6	11.4	4.1	14.6
Limitations in functional capacity:**					
No problems with either ADL or IADL tasks	18.4	10.0	18.6	13.4	39.6
Some problems with IADL, but not ADL, tasks	39.3	12.6	20.2	11.0	16.8
Some problems with ADL, but not IADL, tasks	44.7	10.6	10.6	10.6	23.4
Some problems with both ADL and IADL tasks	52.8	14.8	12.5	5.7	14.2

Note: Only the two extreme values of the scale were labeled.

Note on statistical significance: Significance tests were based on the chi-square statistic for cross-tabulations. Significant differences in the distributions among columns 1 through 5 are denoted by asterisks at the relevant variable: ** denotes statistical significance at the 99 percent level.

[a]Includes siblings-in-law.

Table 7–11
Reported Physical Strain, by Whether Personal Care Is Provided and the Time Devoted to All Care
(percent)

Care Provided by Primary Caregiver	Physical Strain Scale				
	A Great Deal 5	4	3	2	Little or None 1
Personal care:**					
Any personal care provided	32.4	12.3	19.8	11.6	24.0
No personal care provided	10.9	7.8	14.1	13.4	53.8
Average hours per day devoted to all care:[a]**					
One hour or less per day	8.2	4.8	12.6	16.3	58.2
1.01 to 2.00 hours per day	14.3	13.7	17.9	14.3	39.9
2.01 to 4.00 hours per day	18.5	12.0	25.9	13.9	29.6
4.01 to 6.00 hours per day	25.9	11.2	22.8	11.2	28.9
6.01 to 8.00 hours per day	27.3	11.3	16.0	10.0	35.5
More than 8 hours per day	38.8	14.4	17.7	10.2	18.9

Note: Only the two extreme values of the scale were labeled.

Note on statistical significance: Significance tests were based on the chi-square statistic for cross-tabulations. Significant differences in the distributions among columns 1 through 5 are denoted by asterisks at the relevant variable: ** denotes statistical significance at the 99 percent level.

[a]Includes time devoted to socializing.

giving imposed further strains on their health (see table 7–12). Having other persons in the informal network did not appear to reduce the level of physical strain associated with the caregiver's own caregiving efforts. However, reporting that someone was available to provide respite care did appear to lessen the perceived physical strain. The probability of nursing-home placement was positively associated with physical strain, although was less strongly associated with emotional strain.

Financial Strain

Male and female caregivers did not report significantly different levels of financial strain; however, spouses and other caregivers who lived with the care recipient did report higher levels of financial strain than did

Table 7–12
Reported Physical Strain, by Care Alternatives and Other Caregiving Responsibilities
(percent)

Opinion of Primary Caregiver	Physical Strain Scale				
	A Great Deal 5	4	3	2	Little or None 1
Satisfaction with care arrangements					
Caregiver satisfaction with care arrangements:**					
Very satisfied	23.3	8.4	15.9	10.6	41.8
Somewhat satisfied	20.2	14.2	21.4	14.2	30.0
Not too satisfied	39.3	12.7	16.8	10.6	20.7
No other arrangements	28.0	8.4	17.6	13.4	32.6
Worries about sufficient help for care recipient:**					
Quite a lot	34.8	11.3	20.2	11.4	22.4
Sometimes	17.0	11.5	20.2	13.9	37.5
Rarely	16.1	9.7	11.0	15.5	47.7
Not at all	17.7	9.6	10.8	9.6	52.2
Care alternatives available to primary informal caregiver					
Availability of others in network:					
Others in caregiving network	28.7	11.2	16.3	12.1	33.3
No others in caregiving network	24.4	10.9	19.4	12.2	31.5
Availability of respite care, reported by primary caregiver:**					
Someone else available to provide same types of care	17.5	10.4	17.2	13.7	41.2
No one else available to provide same types of care	29.3	11.4	18.7	11.6	29.0
Probability of nursing-home placement within next year:*					
Currently in nursing home	27.9	11.6	16.3	9.3	34.9
Certainly will	39.3	10.7	17.9	8.6	23.6
Probably will	31.8	6.8	13.6	15.9	31.8
Even chance	24.1	12.4	19.5	14.8	29.2
Probably will not	23.2	14.8	19.8	11.4	30.9
Certainly will not	24.2	9.6	18.2	12.1	35.8

Note: Only the two extreme values of the scale were labeled.

Note on statistical significance: Significance tests were based on the chi-square statistic for cross-tabulations. Significant differences in the distributions among columns 1 through 5 are denoted by asterisk(s) at the relevant variable: * denotes statistical significance at the 95 percent level; ** denotes statistical significance at the 99 percent level.

those who lived elsewhere (see table 7–13). It is particularly noteworthy that spouses reported financial strain, given that the channeling study interview did not ask the spouses whether or how much they contributed toward the additional expenses associated with the elderly care recipient's disabilities or poor health.

The perceptions of primary caregivers toward financial strain were not significantly associated with the care recipient's income, and were only weakly associated with insurance coverage (see table 7–14). However, the financial strain experienced by caregivers was significantly correlated with the caregiver's own financial circumstances; caregivers whose total gross household income was less than $1,000 per month and those who contributed more than 20 percent of their own income toward the care recipient's expenses reported higher levels of financial strain.

Table 7–13
Reported Financial Strain, by Caregiver Gender, Relationship to Care Recipient, and Living Arrangement
(percent)

	Financial Strain Scale				
Characteristic of Primary Caregiver	*A Great Deal* 5	4	3	2	*Little or None* 1
Caregiver gender:					
Male	12.6	4.3	14.8	13.0	55.3
Female	12.8	6.3	12.8	9.9	58.1
Relationship to care recipient:**					
Spouse	21.2	8.5	18.6	12.7	39.1
Daughter	14.4	7.1	14.9	10.3	53.2
Son	10.8	4.7	14.2	16.0	54.2
Daughter-in-law	8.3	6.0	10.7	8.3	66.7
Sibling[a]	8.8	2.9	13.1	11.0	64.2
Other	5.2	2.7	6.4	7.3	78.3
Living arrangements:**					
Lives with care recipient					
Spouse	21.2	8.5	18.6	12.5	39.2
Nonspouse	14.7	8.4	15.3	13.1	48.6
Does not live with care recipient	6.9	2.4	9.2	8.1	73.4

Note: Only the two extreme values of the scale were labeled.

Note on statistical significance: Significance tests were based on the chi-square statistic for cross-tabulations. Significant differences in the distributions among columns 1 through 5 are denoted by asterisks at the relevant variable: ** denotes statistical significance at the 99 percent level.

[a]Includes siblings-in-law.

Table 7–14
Reported Financial Strain, by Caregiver and Care Recipient Financial Circumstances
(percent)

	Financial Strain Scale				
	A Great Deal				Little or None
Financial Circumstances	5	4	3	2	1
Caregiver financial circumstances					
Caregiver monthly income:**					
Less than $500	16.6	6.3	8.8	9.1	59.2
$500 to $999	16.5	7.6	15.8	12.6	47.4
$1,000 or more	10.5	5.1	13.7	10.7	59.9
Financial support to care recipient:**					
Provides any	17.1	8.0	20.7	15.4	38.8
Provides none	4.4	2.4	4.3	5.8	83.0
Spouse of care recipient[a]	21.2	8.5	18.6	12.7	39.1
Proportion of caregiver income to financial support:**					
None	10.3	4.5	9.3	8.2	67.6
5 percent or less	6.3	3.6	13.4	14.8	61.9
6 to 10 percent	17.1	6.3	18.0	23.4	35.1
11 to 20 percent	18.5	9.3	31.5	16.7	24.1
Greater than 20 percent	33.3	15.0	23.5	9.8	18.3
Care recipient financial circumstances					
Care recipient monthly income:					
Less than $300	18.0	5.7	13.1	9.8	53.3
$300 to $499	10.6	6.0	13.2	10.8	59.4
$500 to $999	12.7	6.3	13.4	10.2	57.5
$1,000 or more	14.4	3.4	13.9	13.9	54.6
Insurance coverage:*					
Medicaid	16.6	5.6	11.5	8.6	57.8
Medicare, no Medicaid	11.5	5.8	13.9	11.3	57.4
Other	31.6	5.3	5.3	10.5	47.4

Note: Only the two extreme values of the scale were labeled.

Note on statistical significance: Significance tests were based on the chi-square statistic for cross-tabulations. Significant differences in the distributions among columns 1 through 5 are denoted by asterisk(s) at the relevant variable: * denotes statistical significance at the 95 percent level; ** denotes statistical significance at the 99 percent level.

[a]Primary caregivers who were spouses were assumed to share all expenses jointly with the care recipient, and, because of the difficulty they were expected to have in identifying those expenses due specifically to the elderly person's illness or disability, spouses were not included in the definition of financial assistance networks.

General Satisfaction with Life

Caregivers were asked to assess their life in general, independent of the specific context of caregiving. Only about one-fifth (20.7 percent) stated that their lives were "completely satisfying"; 37.7 percent reported that their lives generally were "not very satisfying," and the remaining 41.6 percent stated that their lives were "pretty satisfying." These figures contrast sharply with the findings of several studies of life satisfaction among the general population. Campbell, Converse, and Rodgers (1976, 46) analyzed a similar question on the general satisfaction with life (using a 7-point scale, from completely dissatisfied to completely satisfied), based on data collected in personal interviews during 1971 with a nationally representative sample of 2,164 adults who were 18 years of age or older. In that study, only 6.7 percent of the respondents reported any level of dissatisfaction with their lives. A 1978 NBC News/Associated Press survey found that 28 percent of the respondents were very satisfied with their lives, while 14 percent were only slightly satisfied or not at all satisfied (*Public Opinion* 1979, 22). The 1982 General Social Survey conducted by the National Opinion Research Center included a question on personal happiness—33 percent of the respondents stated that they were very happy, 54 percent fairly happy, and only 13 percent not too happy (*Public Opinion* 1982, 25).

Among caregivers in the channeling demonstration, women were less likely than men to report high levels of satisfaction, and live-in caregivers were also generally less satisfied with their lives than were those who were not live-in caregivers (see table 7–15). Spouses and children who provided care to the elderly also generally reported lower levels of satisfaction than did other caregivers.

All aspects of the strain of caregiving—emotional, physical, and financial—were negatively associated with general life satisfaction (see table 7–16). The strongest of such relationships pertained to emotional strain, and the weakest pertained to financial strain. This finding reinforces the special importance of emotional strain and its link to the stresses of caregiving, as demonstrated earlier in this chapter and in previous studies. Physical and financial strain were experienced less often as part of caregiving responsibilities; they were also less closely associated with the circumstances of caregiving and the limitations it imposed, and exhibited weaker relationships with the perceptions of caregivers about the overall quality of their lives.

Summary

The findings of this chapter support the dominant view in the literature that providing care to elderly persons can be a stressful and sometimes

Table 7–15
General Life Satisfaction, by Caregiver Gender, Relationship to Care Recipient, and Living Arrangement
(percent)

Characteristic of Primary Caregiver	General Life Satisfaction		
	Completely Satisfying	Pretty Satisfying	Not Very Satisfying
Caregiver gender:*			
Male	24.7	39.7	35.6
Female	19.2	42.3	38.5
Relationship to care recipient:**			
Spouse	18.0	37.4	44.6
Daughter	10.8	44.2	44.9
Son	17.5	40.8	41.7
Daughter-in-law	15.1	36.0	48.8
Sibling[a]	28.8	35.2	36.0
Other	36.6	45.5	17.9
Living arrangement:**			
Lives with care recipient			
Spouse	18.1	37.5	44.4
Nonspouse	14.1	40.0	45.9
Does not live with care recipient	27.1	44.9	28.0

Note on statistical significance: Significance tests were based on the chi-square statistic for cross-tabulations. Significant differences in the distributions among columns 1 through 3 are denoted by asterisk(s) at the relevant variable: * denotes statistical significance at the 95 percent level; ** denotes statistical significance at the 99 percent level.
[a]Includes siblings-in-law.

strenuous experience. As reported by family and friends who were engaged in providing care to the elderly in the channeling demonstration, caregiving often directly restricted the opportunities to participate in other activities; moreover, it affected other relationships, and it entailed physical labor and financial sacrifices. The behavior of care recipients can also strain the relationship between the care recipient and the caregiver. Persons who are primarily responsible for providing informal care to the disabled elderly are likely to be concerned about the effectiveness of the total system of care and worried about whether the necessary levels of care will be available. As a result of these circumstances of caregiving, primary caregivers often experience emotional and physical stress and, to some degree, financial strain as well.

The characteristics of the caregivers themselves were also associated with the stress and satisfaction experienced by caregivers. In particular, the stress of caregiving seems to be felt most acutely by female caregivers; male children may, for example, be better able to distance themselves physically and emotionally from their parents when providing informal care (as noted by Robinson and Thurnher 1979, 591). Compounding

Table 7–16
General Life Satisfaction, by Emotional, Physical, and Financial Strain
(percent)

| Type of Strain | General Life Satisfaction | | |
	Completely Satisfying	Pretty Satisfying	Not Very Satisfying
Emotional strain scale:**			
5 — great deal	10.7	27.9	61.3
4	11.2	47.9	40.8
3	16.8	53.4	29.9
2	28.4	54.6	17.0
1 — little or none	47.6	44.3	8.1
Physical strain scale:**			
5 — great deal	8.9	29.0	62.1
4	12.5	39.4	48.1
3	16.1	46.5	37.4
2	16.1	50.4	33.5
1 — little or none	36.7	46.8	16.6
Financial strain scale:**			
5 — great deal	14.9	23.0	62.1
4	12.2	35.5	52.3
3	14.4	38.4	47.2
2	15.4	41.3	43.3
1 — little or none	25.1	47.4	27.5

Note: Only the two extreme values of the scale were labeled.

Note on statistical significance: Significance tests were based on the chi-square statistic for cross-tabulations. Significant differences in the distributions among columns 1 through 3 are denoted by asterisks at the relevant variable: ** denotes statistical significance at the 99 percent level.

the stress experienced by the female caregiver is the apparent unwillingness to share stressful situations with a spouse. Horowitz (1978, 12) observed that the spouses of male caregivers in her case studies were often involved in providing care to their husbands' parents, but that daughters who were providing care to their own parents frequently attempted to minimize the involvement of their husbands in caregiving roles. In the channeling study, those persons who were more likely to provide substantial care—women (particularly wives, daughters, and daughters-in-law) and live-in caregivers—experienced greater strain associated with caregiving than did other groups.

All caregivers strongly resisted the possibility of placing the care recipient in a nursing home, but many caregivers were concerned about the availability of care arrangements, both formal and informal, to provide adequate care to their elderly relative or friend. These caregivers also felt that they were carrying most of the burden alone. Their reports of the probability of nursing-home placement for the care recipients were directly associated with the level of strain they were experiencing. Although these reports cannot be translated precisely into future rates of institutionalization, this result does support the presumption that the level of strain is likely to be an important factor in determining institutionalization rates. Efforts to maximize community-based care for the elderly must take into account the emotional costs of caregiving in the informal support system.

Notes

1. For example, one question read as follows:

"Now, I'm going to read a list of problems people sometimes have when taking care of a disabled person. For each one, please tell me whether it is *true* for you or *not*.

Taking care of (Name of Elderly Person) limits the time you have to spend with your children or other family members."

The question format creates a frame of reference which links the response to the caregiver's actual experience.

2. There were 496 unemployed caregivers who were 70 years of age or older, which represents 25.6 percent of all caregivers who were interviewed for this study.

3. Conversely, at least one study (Zarit, Reever, and Bach-Peterson 1980, 652) has found no association between (1) the burden experienced by persons who provide informal care to elderly persons with senile dementia and (2) the severity of behavioral problems.

4. These questions were originally developed by Dr. Marjorie Cantor of Fordham University's Center on Gerontology, and appeared in the Collateral Questionnaire for the study, "The Impact of the Entry of the Formal Organization on the Existing Informal Networks of Older Americans," April 1979 (Cantor 1979).

Appendixes

Appendix A
Technical Appendix on Survey Nonresponse

A large proportion (87 percent) of the informal caregivers named by the elderly in the channeling caregiver study completed interviews. However, any amount of nonresponse, no matter how small, is reason enough to be concerned about biased study results because of differences between those who responded to the survey and those who did not.

Unlike many other studies, the channeling survey obtained information on nonrespondents. No data are available on the elderly to whom they provided care, as shown in the column labeled "Informal Caregivers Named But Not Interviewed" in table A–1. The elderly whose informal

Table A–1
Comparison of Characteristics of Elderly in Caregiver Study, by Caregiver Interview Completion Status
(percent)

Characteristic of Elderly Person	Informal Caregiver Named but Not Interviewed[a]	Appropriate Informal Caregiver Named and Interviewed
Gender:		
Female	65.7	71.2
Age:		
65 to 74 years	28.4	26.9
75 to 79 years	21.8	20.7
80 to 84 years	25.6	22.6
Older than 84 years	24.2	29.8
Ethnic background:		
Black	23.2	23.9
Hispanic	5.9	3.8
White or other[b]	70.9	72.3
Marital status:		
Now married	38.1	32.8
Not presently married	61.9	67.2
Living situation:**		
Alone	36.3	33.0
With spouse	37.4	31.9
With child	14.5	23.8
With others	11.8	11.3

Table A–1
continued

Characteristic of Elderly Person	Informal Caregiver Named but Not Interviewed[a]	Appropriate Informal Caregiver Named and Interviewed
Monthly income:		
Less than $300	13.5	12.8
$300 to $499	38.9	40.4
$500 to $999	35.8	35.8
$1,000 or more	11.8	11.1
Insurance coverage:		
Medicaid	24.6	19.7
Medicare, no Medicaid	74.0	79.3
Other	1.4	1.0
Impairment of ADL:		
Eating	24.2	27.0
Toileting	58.1	57.0
Bathing	78.2	78.7
Transfer	55.0	52.0
Dressing	57.1	61.3
Impairment in continence	47.8	53.8
Impairment of IADL:		
Use of telephone	51.2	55.6
Money management*	68.4	74.7
Traveling	86.5	88.8
Housework	96.9	97.5
Meal preparation*	85.0	89.2
Shopping	97.5	96.1
Taking medicine*	55.9	63.0
Impairment of mental ability:[c]		
Severe	31.8	32.7
Moderate	38.8	38.6
Mild	29.4	28.7

Note on statistical significance: Significance tests were based on the chi-square statistic for cross-tabulations. Significant differences in the distributions between columns are denoted by asterisks at the relevant variable: * denotes statistical significance at the 95 percent level; ** denotes statistical significance at the 99 percent level.

[a]Sample sizes vary, due to missing data, from 201 to 289 for the named but not interviewed column and from 1,271 to 1,940 for the named and interviewed column.

[b]All those of Hispanic origin are reported in that category; other includes native Americans, Alaskan natives, Asians, or Pacific Islanders (totaling less than 1 percent of the sample).

[c]Measured by the Short Portable Mental Status Questionnaire (SPMSQ), a 10-question test of mental functioning. Severe impairment was indicated by zero to five correct answers out of ten possible, moderate impairment by six to eight correct answers, and mild impairment by nine to ten correct answers.

caregivers were not interviewed were generally not significantly different from those whose caregivers did complete interviews. The only major difference between the two groups of elderly pertained to their living arrangements; elderly persons whose caregivers were not interviewed were more likely to have been living alone or only with their spouses than were the elderly whose caregivers completed the interview. This finding probably reflects, in the first instance, the greater difficulty associated with locating and scheduling appointments with caregivers who did not live with the elderly person, and, in the second, problems associated with conducting interviews with another, possibly frail, elderly person. A few statistically significant differences in IADL impairments were also found: the elderly whose primary caregivers were not interviewed were somewhat less likely to have been impaired in some of these activities.

Appendix B
Survey Instrument

OMB APPROVAL NO: 0990-0102
EXPIRES: NOVEMBER 30, 1983
MPRI: 783

NATIONAL LONG TERM CARE

DEMONSTRATION

Informal Caregiver Survey Baseline

Mathematica Policy Research
January, 1983

Informal Caregiver Survey Baseline

Table of Contents

USE THIS INTRODUCTION IF THE CAREGIVER
RESPONDENT DID NOT SIGN THE BASELINE CONSENT FORM
FOR THE SAMPLE MEMBER

Good (morning/afternoon/evening). I'm _____ with Mathematica
Policy Research in Princeton, New Jersey. As you (may) know, we are doing
a study for the Department of Health and Human Services to learn about the
different kinds of help ill and disabled older people receive from
relatives and friends. The information will be used to improve programs
for older people and the relatives and friends who care for them. (As you
(may) know,) Your name has been given to us by (SAMPLE MEMBER/PROXY/
SIGNIFICANT OTHER/GUARDIAN), as a friend or family member who helps (SAMPLE
MEMBER/him/her) a great deal. I would like to ask you some questions about
the ways that you help (SAMPLE MEMBER).

While your participation is extremely important to the overall accuracy of
the study, the survey is completely voluntary. Whether you choose to
participate or not, will not affect the Social Security benefits or
benefits from any other program received by anyone in your household or in
SAMPLE MEMBER'S household.

This study is authorized by the Older Americans Act, the Social Security
Act, and the Public Health Services Act. Your name and answers will be
kept completely confidential, in accordance with the Privacy Act of 1974.

My questions will take about thirty minutes. I'd like to begin now.

USE THIS INTRODUCTION IF
THE CAREGIVER RESPONDENT SIGNED
THE BASELINE CONSENT FORM

Good (morning/afternoon/evening). I'm _____ and I'm with
Mathematica Policy Research in Princeton, New Jersey. You may remember
that we are doing a study for the Department of Health and Human Services
to learn about the different types of help disabled older people receive
from their families and friends. The information will be used to design
better programs to help older people and the family members and friends who
care for them.

When you signed a form recently to allow SAMPLE MEMBER to participate in
the study you said that you were the friend or family member who helped
(him/her) the most. Now, I would like to ask you some questions about the
ways that you help (him/her).

While your participation is extremely important to the overall accuracy of
the study, the survey is completely voluntary. Whether you choose to
participate or not, will not affect the Social Security benefits or
benefits from any other program received by anyone in your household or in
SAMPLE MEMBER'S household.

This study is authorized by the Older Americans Act, the Social Security
Act, and the Public Health Services Act. Your name and answers will be
kept completely confidential, in accordance with the Privacy Act of 1974.

My questions will take about thirty minutes. I'd like to begin now.

SAMPLE MEMBER'S ID: |___|___|-|___|___|___|___|___|-|___|

```
┌─────────────────────────────────────────────────────────────┐
│ INTERVIEWER:  IS THIS THE PRIMARY CAREGIVER NAMED ON THE ELDERLY │
│               SAMPLE MEMBER'S BASELINE CONSENT FORM OR WAS THE   │
│               SAMPLE MEMBER RECONTACTED?                         │
│                                                                 │
│               NAME ON CONSENT FORM . . . . . . . . . 01         │
│                                                                 │
│               RECONTACT  . . . . . . . . . . . . . . 02         │
└─────────────────────────────────────────────────────────────┘
```

```
┌──────────────────────────────────────────────────┐
│                                    AM . . . 01     │
│  START TIME:  |___|___|:|___|___|                  │
│                                    PM . . . 02     │
└──────────────────────────────────────────────────┘
```

S. SCREEN

S1. CODE WITHOUT ASKING IF KNOWN.
     Are you related to <u>SAMPLE MEMBER</u>?

IF YES: How?

IF NO: Are you a
         friend or
         an employee?

SPOUSE	01 (S3)
DAUGHTER	02 (S3)
SON.	03 (S3)
SISTER	04 (S3)
BROTHER.	05 (S3)
PARENT	06 (S3)
DAUGHTER-IN-LAW.	07 (S3)
SON-IN-LAW	08 (S3)
SISTER-IN-LAW.	09 (S3)
BROTHER-IN-LAW	10 (S3)
GRANDCHILD	11 (S3)
OTHER RELATIVE	12 (S3)
FRIEND OR NEIGHBOR	13 (S3)
EMPLOYEE OF SAMPLE MEMBER.	14
EMPLOYEE OR VOLUNTEER FROM ORGANIZATION.	15
NOT ANSWERED	-1 (E28)

S2. When we spoke to (SAMPLE MEMBER/<u>SIGNATORY</u>) recently, (he/she) named you as
     the <u>friend or family member</u> who helped (<u>SAMPLE MEMBER</u>/him/her) the most day
     to day. Were you a friend of <u>SAMPLE MEMBER</u>, <u>before</u> you were employed to
     help take care of (him/her)?

PROBE: By friend I mean
        something <u>more</u> than
        an acquaintance.

SEE CT9 FOR NAME OF
RESPONDENT FOR SAMPLE
MEMBER BASELINE.

YES, FRIEND BEFORE 01	
NO 02 (E28)	
NOT ANSWERED . . . .-1 (E28)	

- 1 -

```
               HELP WITH THE FOLLOWING TASKS IS INCLUDED


MEDICAL CARE
   GIVING MEDICINES OR INJECTIONS
   PHYSICAL, OCCUPATIONAL, OR SPEECH THERAPY
   OTHER MEDICAL TREATMENTS

PERSONAL CARE
   EATING
   GETTING OUT OF BED OR A CHAIR
   DRESSING
   BATHING
   GETTING TO OR USING THE TOILET
   CLEANING UP AFTER BLADDER OR BOWEL ACCIDENTS

MEAL PREPARATION

HOUSEWORK

LAUNDRY

SHOPPING

CHORES (HEAVY HOUSEWORK AND MINOR REPAIRS)

TRANSPORTATION AND ESCORT

MANAGING FINANCIAL AFFAIRS

MONITORING (SUPERVISION FOR PERSONAL SAFETY)

ARRANGING FOR BENEFITS OR SERVICES AND DEALING WITH SERVICE
   PROVIDERS

MINOR ERRANDS
```

S3. CODE WITHOUT ASKING IF KNOWN.
Is <u>SAMPLE MEMBER</u> at home now or in a hospital or nursing home?

AT HOME. 01 (S7)

HOSPITAL 02

NURSING HOME 03

SM DECEASED. 04 (S12)

NOT ANSWERED . . . .-1

S4. Did you regularly help <u>SAMPLE MEMBER</u> to take care of (himself/herself) or (his/her) affairs, or to do things around the house in the month before (he/she) entered the (hospital/nursing home)?

REGULARLY = ON A ROUTINE
BASIS WITH HELP PROVIDED
AT LEAST ONCE A MONTH.

YES. 01 (S15)

NO 02

NOT ANSWERED . . . .-1

S5. Did you regularly help (him/her) in some other way in the month before (he/she) entered the (hospital/nursing) home?

YES. . . . . .01 ──▶ Could you describe that?

NO 02   _____

NOT ANSWERED . . . .-1   _____

_____

S6. | INTERVIEWER: DID THE RESPONDENT <u>REGULARLY</u> HELP THE SAMPLE MEMBER AT THAT TIME WITH ONE OR MORE OF THE INCLUDED TASKS? (SEE S5 AND THE CHART ON THE OPPOSITE PAGE)

YES 01 (S15)

NO 02 (E28)

S5 NOT ANSWERED. 03 (E28)

S7. Do you regularly help <u>SAMPLE MEMBER</u> now to take care of (himself/herself) or (his/ her) affairs, or to do things around the house?

YES. 01 (S17)

NO 02

NOT ANSWERED . . . .-1

- 3 -

HELP WITH THE FOLLOWING TASKS IS <u>INCLUDED</u>

MEDICAL CARE
  GIVING MEDICINES OR INJECTIONS
  PHYSICAL, OCCUPATIONAL, OR SPEECH THERAPY
  OTHER MEDICAL TREATMENTS

PERSONAL CARE
  EATING
  GETTING OUT OF BED OR A CHAIR
  DRESSING
  BATHING
  GETTING TO OR USING THE TOILET
  CLEANING UP AFTER BLADDER OR BOWEL ACCIDENTS

MEAL PREPARATION

HOUSEWORK

LAUNDRY

SHOPPING

CHORES (HEAVY HOUSEWORK AND MINOR REPAIRS)

TRANSPORTATION AND ESCORT

MANAGING FINANCIAL AFFAIRS

MONITORING (SUPERVISION FOR PERSONAL SAFETY)

ARRANGING FOR BENEFITS OR SERVICES AND DEALING WITH SERVICE
    PROVIDERS

MINOR ERRANDS

S8. Do you regularly help (him/her) in some other way now?

> YES . . . . . 01 ────▶ Could you describe that?
>
> NO. . . . . . 02 _____
>
> NOT ANSWERED. -1 _____
> REGULARLY = ON A
> ROUTINE BASIS WITH _____
> HELP PROVIDED AT
> LEAST ONCE A MONTH.

S9. INTERVIEWER: DOES THE RESPONDENT <u>REGULARLY</u> HELP THE SAMPLE MEMBER NOW WITH ONE OR MORE OF THE INCLUDED TASKS?

(SEE S8 AND THE CHART ON THE OPPOSITE PAGE.)

> YES 01 (S17)
>
> NO 02
>
> S8 NOT ANSWERED . . . 03

S10. In the past, did you regularly help <u>SAMPLE MEMBER</u> to take care of (himself/herself) or (his/her) affairs, or to do things around the house?

IF NO, REFER TO CHART: YES, HELPED IN PAST. 01
Did you regularly help   (CHECK IDENTITY
(him/her) in some other   NO, NEVER HELPED . . . . .02 ──▶ OF R. IF CORRECT
way?   R, E28)

NOT ANSWERED . . . .-1

S11. CODE WITHOUT ASKING IF KNOWN.
Why aren't you helping (him/her) now?

IF SOMEONE ELSE HELPS   SOMEONE ELSE HELPS NOW 01 (S13)
NOW, PROBE FOR WHETHER
RESPONDENT HAS BEEN ILL   SM LIVES WITH SOMEONE ELSE/
OR AWAY.   SOMEWHERE ELSE NOW 02 (S13)

SM IS IN NURSING HOME/HOSPITAL
   NOW OR WAS DISCHARGED RECENTLY 03 (S14)

SM HAS DIED 04

RESPONDENT IS OR HAS BEEN ILL RECENTLY .05 (S13)

RESPONDENT HAS BEEN AWAY RECENTLY. . . .06 (S13)

RESPONDENT MOVED 07 (S13)

OTHER (SPECIFY)_____ 08 (S13)

_____
                                    QC ONLY

NOT ANSWERED . . . .-1 (S13)

S12. I'm very sorry to hear that. When did (he/she) die?

DATE OF DEATH . . |___|___| |___|___| |___|___| (E29)
MONTH DAY YEAR

NOT ANSWERED . . . .-1 (E29)

S13. When were you last helping SAMPLE MEMBER regularly? Was it within the past month?

REGULARLY = ON A ROUTINE
BASIS WITH HELP PROVIDED
AT LEAST ONCE A MONTH.

YES, WITHIN PAST MONTH . . .01 (S15)

NO, MORE THAN ONE
 MONTH AGO. 02 (E28)

NOT ANSWERED . . . .-1 (E28)

S14. Were you helping SAMPLE MEMBER regularly in the month before (he/she) entered the (hospital/nursing home)?

YES. 01

NO 02 (E28)

NOT ANSWERED . . . .-1 (E28)

S15. (I/Someone) spoke with SAMPLE MEMBER (or someone else who answered for (him/her)) on DATE OF SAMPLE MEMBER BASELINE. Please think about SAMPLE MEMBER'S health then as compared with (his/her) health when you were last helping (him/her) regularly.

Would you say that (his/her) health in general was better, worse or about the same on DATE as when you were last helping (him/her) regularly?

SEE CT10 FOR DATE OF
SAMPLE MEMBER BASELINE.

BETTER ON DATE THAN WHEN LAST HELPING . . . 01

WORSE ON DATE THAN WHEN LAST HELPING. . . . 02

ABOUT THE SAME. 03

NOT ANSWERED. . . . . -1

S16. INTERVIEWER: IN SECTIONS A-D, ASK ABOUT THE PERIOD WHEN THE RESPONDENT WAS LAST HELPING THE SAMPLE MEMBER REGULARLY.

*** ALL SKIP TO A1. ***

S17. INTERVIEWER: IN SECTIONS A-D, ASK ABOUT HELP RESPONDENT GIVES TO SAMPLE MEMBER NOW.

- 6 -

```
DECIMAL FRACTIONS OF AN HOUR:

    5 MINUTES                         30 MINUTES = 00.5 HOURS
       OR LESS = 00.1 HOURS
                                      35 MINUTES = 00.6 HOURS
   10 MINUTES = 00.2 HOURS
                                      45 MINUTES = 00.8 HOURS
   15 MINUTES = 00.2 HOURS
                                      50 MINUTES = 00.8 HOURS
   20 MINUTES = 00.3 HOURS
                                      55 MINUTES = 00.9 HOURS
   25 MINUTES = 00.4 HOURS



MONTH CODES:

        JANUARY . . . . . . 01        JULY. . . . . . . . 07

        FEBRUARY. . . . . . 02        AUGUST  . . . . . . 08

        MARCH . . . . . . . 03        SEPTEMBER . . . . . 09

        APRIL . . . . . . . 04        OCTOBER . . . . . . 10

        MAY . . . . . . . . 05        NOVEMBER  . . . . . 11

        JUNE  . . . . . . . 06        DECEMBER  . . . . . 12
```

A. CARE BY PRIMARY INFORMAL CAREGIVER

A1.   CODE WITHOUT ASKING IF KNOWN:

(Do/Did) you live with <u>SAMPLE MEMBER</u> (at the time you were last helping (him/her) regularly)?

PROBE: Just before (he/she)   (LIVES/LIVED) WITH 01 (A3)
            entered the (hospital/
            nursing home) (this/   (DOES/DID) NOT LIVE WITH 02
            last) time,
            Just before (he/she)   NOT ANSWERED . . . .-1 (A3)
            moved,
            Just before you (became
            ill/went out-of-town)?

REGULARLY = ON A ROUTINE
BASIS WITH HELP PROVIDED
AT LEAST ONCE A MONTH.

A2.   About how long (does/did) it take you to get from your house to where <u>SAMPLE MEMBER</u> (is/was) living?

                                               SEE CODES OPPOSITE.

PROBE: The way you usually   HOURS. . . . . . . |___|___|.|___|
            (go/went when you
            were last helping   NOT ANSWERED . . . .-1
            regularly)?

A3.   How often (do/did) you regularly help <u>SAMPLE MEMBER</u> (at that time)?

                                          PER WEEK . . 01
PROBE: On the average?   DAYS . . |___|___|➤
REGULARLY = ON A ROUTINE   PER MONTH. . 02
BASIS WITH HELP PROVIDED
AT LEAST ONCE A MONTH.   LESS THAN ONE DAY PER MONTH . . 00 ➤(REVIEW
                                                  SCREEN)
           NOT ANSWERED . . . .-1

A4.   When did you start spending as much time taking care of (him/her) as you (do now/did when you were last helping regularly)?

PROBE: As you did just before YEAR . . . . .19|___|___|
            (he/she) entered the
            (hospital/nursing   NOT ANSWERED . . . . -1 (A6)
            home) (this/last)
            time,
            As you did just before
            (he/she) moved,
            As you did just before
            you (became ill/went
            out-of-town)?

```
MONTH CODES:

JANUARY . . . . . . 01      JULY. . . . . . . . 07

FEBRUARY. . . . . . 02      AUGUST  . . . . . . 08

MARCH . . . . . . . 03      SEPTEMBER . . . . . 09

APRIL . . . . . . . 04      OCTOBER . . . . . . 10

MAY . . . . . . . . 05      NOVEMBER  . . . . . 11

JUNE  . . . . . . . 06      DECEMBER  . . . . . 12
```

A5.   IF CURRENT OR PREVIOUS YEAR IN A4:
      In what month was that?

                                                    SEE CODES OPPOSITE.

                              MONTH. . . . . |__|__|

                              NOT ANSWERED . . . . -1

```
┌─────────────────────────────────────────────────────────────────────┐
│  A6.   INTERVIEWER:  (DOES/DID) THE RESPONDENT LIVE WITH SAMPLE MEMBER?│
│        (IS A1 CODED "01"?)                                             │
│                                                                       │
│                          YES. . . . . . . . . . . . . . .01 (A8)      │
│                                                                       │
│                          NO . . . . . . . . . . . . . . .02           │
│                                                                       │
│                          A1 NOT ANSWERED. . . . . . . . .03 (A8)      │
└─────────────────────────────────────────────────────────────────────┘
```

A7.   About how long (do/did) you stay on an average day?

      PROBE: An average day when   HOURS. . . . . . . |__|__|.|__|
               you (are helping/
               were last helping   NOT ANSWERED . . . .-1
               regularly)?

      IF MULTIPLE VISITS PER DAY:
      COUNT ALL VISITS IN ONE DAY

```
┌─────────────────────────────────────────────────────────────────────┐
│  DECIMAL FRACTIONS OF AN HOUR:                                        │
│                                                                       │
│        5 MINUTES                      30 MINUTES = 00.5 HOURS          │
│           OR LESS = 00.1 HOURS                                        │
│                                       35 MINUTES = 00.6 HOURS          │
│       10 MINUTES = 00.2 HOURS                                         │
│                                       45 MINUTES = 00.8 HOURS          │
│       15 MINUTES = 00.2 HOURS                                         │
│                                       50 MINUTES = 00.8 HOURS          │
│       20 MINUTES = 00.3 HOURS                                         │
│                                       55 MINUTES = 00.9 HOURS          │
│       25 MINUTES = 00.4 HOURS                                         │
└─────────────────────────────────────────────────────────────────────┘
```

A8. Now, I'm going to mention some things about medical and personal care that people sometimes need help with. For each, please tell me whether you <u>regularly</u> help(ed) <u>SAMPLE MEMBER</u> with that (now/when you were last helping (him/her)).

INCLUDE SUPERVISION IN THE SAME ROOM AS ASSISTANCE.
REGULARLY = ON A ROUTINE BASIS WITH HELP PROVIDED AT LEAST ONCE A MONTH.

IF YES ─────────────────────→

PROBE: On the days you help(ed),

<u>YES</u> <u>NO</u> <u>NA</u>

a. (Do/Did) you regularly help (him/her) take medicine or give (him/her) injections? . . . . 01 02 −1

   PROBE: Shots?
           On the days you help(ed)?

b. (Do/Did) you regularly help with physical, occupational or speech therapy? . 01 02 −1

   PROBE: For example, by supervising exercises?

c. (Do/Did) you regularly help with <u>other</u> medical treatments, like giving oxygen or changing bandages?. . . . . 01 02 −1

d. (Do/Did) you regularly feed (him/her) or help (him/her) eat? . . . . 01 02 −1

   EXCLUDE CUTTING MEAT OR BUTTERING BREAD.

e. (Do/Did) you regularly help (him/her) get out of bed or a chair? . . . . . . 01 02 −1

f. (Do/Did) you regularly help (him/her) dress, by getting clothes or helping put them on?. . . . . 01 02 −1

   PROBE: Or change (his/her) nightclothes?

g. (Do/Did) you regularly help (him/her) bathe, in a tub or shower, at a sink or basin, or in bed? . . . . 01 02 −1

   INCLUDE HELP IN GETTING IN AND OUT OF TUB OR SHOWER.

h. (Do/Did) you regularly help (him/her) get to, or use the toilet,<u>or</u> help with a bedpan, catheter or colostomy bag? . . . . 01 02 −1

   INCLUDE STAYING NEARBY AS ASSISTANCE IN TOILETING. INCLUDE BEDSIDE COMMODE AND CHANGING DIAPERS.

i. (Do/Did) you regularly clean up after bladder or bowel accidents?. . . . . . 01 02 −1

```
                                          ↓     ↓
                                   ┌──────────────────┐
                                   │ GO TO BOTTOM OF   │
                                   │   NEXT PAGE       │
                                   └──────────────────┘
```

A9. About how many times (do/did) you
help with that on an average day?

　　PROBE: On an average day when you
　　　　　(are helping/were last
　　　　　helping regularly)?

IF LESS THAN ONCE PER DAY:

A9.1 　　About how often did you do that?

	EVERY 2–4 DAYS	EVERY 5–7 DAYS/ ONCE A WK	LESS THAN THAT	NA
a. MEDICINE　TIMES . . |___|___|				
LESS THAN ONCE. .-4 ⟶	01	02	03	-1
NA. . . . .-1				
b. THERAPY　TIMES . . |___|___|				
LESS THAN ONCE. .-4 ⟶	01	02	03	-1
NA. . . . .-1				
c. MEDICAL TREATMENTS　TIMES . . |___|___|				
LESS THAN ONCE. .-4 ⟶	01	02	03	-1
NA. . . . .-1				
d. EATING　TIMES . . |___|___|				
LESS THAN ONCE. .-4 ⟶	01	02	03	-1
NA. . . . .-1				
e. GETTING OUT OF BED OR A CHAIR　TIMES . . |___|___|				
LESS THAN ONCE. .-4 ⟶	01	02	03	-1
NA. . . . .-1				
f. DRESSING　TIMES . . |___|___|				
LESS THAN ONCE. .-4 ⟶	01	02	03	-1
NA. . . . .-1				
g. BATHING　TIMES . . |___|___|				
LESS THAN ONCE. .-4 ⟶	01	02	03	-1
NA. . . . .-1				
h. USING THE TOILET　TIMES . . |___|___|				
LESS THAN ONCE. .-4 ⟶	01	02	03	-1
NA. . . . .-1				
i. CLEANING UP AFTER ACCIDENTS　TIMES . . |___|___|				
LESS THAN ONCE. .-4 ⟶	01	02	03	-1
NA. . . . .-1				

```
READ IF ANY "YES" RESPONSES TO A8; OTHERWISE SKIP TO A11.
```

Before we turn to the other things you do for SAMPLE MEMBER, I'd like to ask how much time
you (spend/spent) in an average day helping with TASKS NAMED IN A8.

A10.   About how many hours on an average day would you say you (spend/spent)
        doing __just__ these things?

        PROBE: On an average day   HOURS PER DAY . . . |___|___|·|___|
                when you (are
                helping/were last   NOT ANSWERED . . . .-1
                helping regularly)?

┌───┐
│ DECIMAL FRACTIONS OF AN HOUR: │
│   │
│   5 MINUTES   30 MINUTES = 00.5 HOURS   │
│   OR LESS = 00.1 HOURS   │
│   │
│   10 MINUTES = 00.2 HOURS   35 MINUTES = 00.6 HOURS   │
│   │
│   15 MINUTES = 00.2 HOURS   45 MINUTES = 00.8 HOURS   │
│   │
│   20 MINUTES = 00.3 HOURS   50 MINUTES = 00.8 HOURS   │
│   │
│   25 MINUTES = 00.4 HOURS   55 MINUTES = 00.9 HOURS   │
└───┘

A11.   The next questions are about helping SAMPLE MEMBER by doing things
        around the house.

        IF LIVING WITH SM: These questions may not seem to apply to you, but
        it's important that we get complete answers from everyone.

        REGULARLY = ON A ROUTINE BASIS WITH HELP
        PROVIDED AT LEAST ONCE A MONTH.

			YES	NO	NA
MEAL PREPARATION	a.	(Do/Did) you regularly fix meals or prepare special foods for (him/her) (when you were last helping)?	01	02	-1
LAUNDRY OR HOUSEWORK	b.	(Do/Did) you regularly do (his/her) laundry or day-to-day housework (around (his/her) home)?	01	02	-1
SHOPPING	c.	Shop for (his/her) food or clothing or for other things (he/she) uses?	01	02	-1
CHORES	d.	Do chores, like washing windows or making minor repairs, (around (his/her) home)? . .	01	02	-1
TRANS-PORTATION	e.	Drive (him/her) places or help (him/her) with using transportation?	01	02	-1
MONEY MANAGEMENT	f.	Help (him/her) manage (his/her) money, for example, by writing checks or paying bills?.	01	02	-1

A12.   INTERVIEWER: DID THE RESPONDENT HELP WITH ANY OF THE TASKS
        IN A11? (IS ANY PART OF A11 ANSWERED "YES"?)

                           YES. 01

                           NO 02 (A18)

                           A11 NOT ANSWERED 03 (A18)

A13.   On an average day about how much time would you say you (spend/spent) on
        TASKS NAMED IN A11?

              PROBE: An average day when   HOURS PER DAY. . . . |___|___|.|___|
                      you (are helping/
                      were last helping   NOT ANSWERED . . . .-1
                      regularly)?

        DECIMAL FRACTIONS OF AN HOUR:

             5 MINUTES   30 MINUTES = 00.5 HOURS
                OR LESS = 00.1 HOURS
                                               35 MINUTES = 00.6 HOURS
            10 MINUTES = 00.2 HOURS
                                               45 MINUTES = 00.8 HOURS
            15 MINUTES = 00.2 HOURS
                                               50 MINUTES = 00.8 HOURS
            20 MINUTES = 00.3 HOURS
                                               55 MINUTES = 00.9 HOURS
            25 MINUTES = 00.4 HOURS

A14.   (Is/Was) any of that time, <u>extra</u> time over and above what you would (spend/have spent) if <u>SAMPLE MEMBER</u> weren't ill or disabled?

YES 01

NO. 02 (A16)

DON'T KNOW. . . . . -1 (A16)

A15.   About what proportion of the <u>TIME IN A13</u> you (spend/spent) on an average day, would you say (is/was) <u>extra</u> time?

PROBE: Your best estimate   PROPORTION . . . . . . |__|__|__| %
        will be fine.

        Time over and above   NOT ANSWERED . . . . -1
        what you would (spend/
        have spent) if (he/
        she) weren't ill or
        disabled?

A16.   INTERVIEWER: DOES THE RESPONDENT DRIVE OR ESCORT THE SAMPLE MEMBER? (IS A11e ANSWERED "YES"?)

YES. 01

NO 02 (A18)

A11e NOT ANSWERED. 03 (A18)

A17.   You said that you (drive/drove) <u>SAMPLE MEMBER</u> places or (help/helped) (him/her) use transportation. About how often (do/did) you do that?

ROUND TRIP = 1 TRIP   TRIPS . . . . . |__|__|__| →   PER WEEK . . . 01

                                                         PER MONTH. . . 02

NOT ANSWERED. . . . . -1

A18.   (Do/When you were last helping regularly, did) you get information about services or benefits for (him/her) or make arrangements for services or benefits on (his/her) behalf?

GETTING INFORMATION AND   YES 01
MAKING ARRANGEMENTS NEED
<u>NOT</u> be DONE REGULARLY.   NO. 02 (A20)

DON'T KNOW. . . . . -1 (A20)

A19.   About how often (do/did) you get information or make arrangements for
        services or benefits?

                                    TIMES. . . |___|___| →   PER WEEK . . . 01
                                                                PER MONTH. . . 02
                                                                PER YEAR . . . 03

                                    LESS THAN ONCE A YEAR 00

                                    NOT ANSWERED . . . .-1

A20.   (Can/Could) SAMPLE MEMBER be left alone at home (when you were last
        helping regularly)?

                                    YES 01 (A22)

                                    NO. 02

                                    NOT ANSWERED . . . . . . -1

A21.   (Do/Did) you regularly stay around so that SAMPLE MEMBER (will/would)
        not be left alone?

        REGULARLY = ON A ROUTINE   YES 01
                    BASIS WITH HELP PROVIDED
                    AT LEAST ONCE A MONTH. NO. 02

                                            NOT ANSWERED . . . . . . -1

A22.   In addition to helping with the kinds of things we've been talking
        about, people often just keep others company, for example, by sitting
        and talking or watching TV. (Do/Did) you regularly do that (when you
        were last helping)?

                                    YES 01

                                    NO. 02 (A24)

                                    NOT ANSWERED. . . . . . . -1 (A24)

A23.   On an average day about how much time (do/did) you spend just keeping
SAMPLE MEMBER company?

        PROBE: An average day when   HOURS PER DAY . . . |___|___|.|___|
                  you (are helping/
                  were last helping
                  regularly)?
                                            NOT ANSWERED . . . .-1

DECIMAL FRACTIONS OF AN HOUR:

        5 MINUTES   30 MINUTES = 00.5 HOURS
            OR LESS = 00.1 HOURS
                                        35 MINUTES = 00.6 HOURS
        10 MINUTES = 00.2 HOURS
                                        45 MINUTES = 00.8 HOURS
        15 MINUTES = 00.2 HOURS
                                        50 MINUTES = 00.8 HOURS
        20 MINUTES = 00.3 HOURS
                                        55 MINUTES = 00.9 HOURS
        25 MINUTES = 00.4 HOURS

A24.   Besides SAMPLE MEMBER (are/were) you helping to care for anyone else
with a long term illness or disability (when you were last helping
SAMPLE MEMBER regularly)?

        REGULARLY = ON A ROUTINE   YES 01
                    BASIS WITH HELP PROVIDED
                    AT LEAST ONCE A MONTH.   NO. 02

                                         DON'T KNOW. . . . . -1

B. CARE FROM OTHER INFORMAL CAREGIVERS

B1. (Next/Still thinking about when you were last helping SAMPLE MEMBER), please tell me the names of friends or family members besides yourself, who regularly help(ed) SAMPLE MEMBER to take care of (himself/ herself) or (his/her) affairs, or who (do/did) things around the house for (him/her).

Please do not include employees, paid or volunteer workers from agencies or organizations, and people who just (come/came) to keep SAMPLE MEMBER company.

PROBE: Anyone else?

IF MORE THAN 4 NAMED: I have some questions about the four of these who help(ed) the most. Who (are/were) they?

REGULARLY = ON A ROUTINE BASIS WITH HELP PROVIDED AT LEAST ONCE A MONTH.

RECORD FIRST NAME ONLY ON GRID.

ASK B2 - B11 FOR
EACH CAREGIVER

NAME 1 _____

DON'T KNOW IF OTHERS HELP. -1 (B12)

NO OTHERS . . . . -4 (B12)

B2. CODE WITHOUT ASKING IF KNOWN. How is NAME related to SAMPLE MEMBER? SEE CODES OPPOSITE.	RELATIONSHIP . . . . |__|__| NOT ANSWERED . . . . . . -1
B3. CODE WITHOUT ASKING IF KNOWN: And is NAME male or female?	MALE. . . . . 01 FEMALE. . . . . 02 NOT ANSWERED. . . . . . -1
B4. (Does/Did) NAME live with SAMPLE MEMBER (when you were last helping regularly)?	(LIVES/LIVED) WITH . . . 01 (DOES/DID) NOT LIVE WITH. 02 NOT ANSWERED. . . . . . . -1
B5. About how often (does/ did) NAME regularly help SAMPLE MEMBER? PROBE: On the average?	|__|__|→ PER WEEK. . . 01 DAYS → PER MONTH . . 02 NA . . . .-1 CONTINUE WITH B6, NEXT PAGE

- 20 -

```
                    RELATIONSHIP CODES
    SPOUSE . . . . . . . . . . . . . . . . . 01
    DAUGHTER . . . . . . . . . . . . . . . . 02
    SON. . . . . . . . . . . . . . . . . . . 03
    SISTER . . . . . . . . . . . . . . . . . 04
    BROTHER. . . . . . . . . . . . . . . . . 05
    PARENT . . . . . . . . . . . . . . . . . 06
    DAUGHTER-IN-LAW. . . . . . . . . . . . . 07
    SON-IN-LAW . . . . . . . . . . . . . . . 08
    SISTER-IN-LAW. . . . . . . . . . . . . . 09
    BROTHER-IN-LAW . . . . . . . . . . . . . 10
    GRANDCHILD . . . . . . . . . . . . . . . 11
    OTHER RELATIVE . . . . . . . . . . . . . 12
    FRIEND OR NEIGHBOR . . . . . . . . . . . 13
          CODES 14 AND 15 NOT APPLICABLE
```

NAME 2 _____   NAME 3 _____   NAME 4 _____

NAME 2	NAME 3	NAME 4
RELATIONSHIP . . . . |__|__| NOT ANSWERED . . . . -1	RELATIONSHIP . . . . |__|__| NOT ANSWERED . . . . -1	RELATIONSHIP . . . . |__|__| NOT ANSWERED . . . . -1
MALE. . . . . 01 FEMALE. . . . . 02 NOT ANSWERED. . . . . . -1	MALE. . . . . 01 FEMALE. . . . . 02 NOT ANSWERED. . . . . . -1	MALE. . . . . 01 FEMALE. . . . . 02 NOT ANSWERED. . . . . . -1
(LIVES/LIVED) WITH. . . . 01 (DOES/DID) NOT LIVE WITH. 02 NOT ANSWERED. . . . . . -1	(LIVES/LIVED) WITH. . . . 01 (DOES/DID) NOT LIVE WITH. 02 NOT ANSWERED. . . . . . -1	(LIVES/LIVED) WITH. . . . 01 (DOES/DID) NOT LIVE WITH. 02 NOT ANSWERED. . . . . . -1
|__|__| → PER WEEK. . . 01 DAYS PER MONTH . . 02 NA . . . . -1 CONTINUE WITH B6, NEXT PAGE	|__|__| → PER WEEK. . . 01 DAYS PER MONTH . . 02 NA . . . . -1 CONTINUE WITH B6, NEXT PAGE	|__|__| → PER WEEK. . . 01 DAYS PER MONTH . . 02 NA . . . . -1 CONTINUE WITH B6, NEXT PAGE

B6.　(Does/Did) <u>NAME</u> <u>regularly</u> help <u>SAMPLE MEMBER</u> --

NAME 1 _____

		YES	NO	NA
a.	with taking medicines, or with medical treatments or therapies?	01	02	-1
b.	with personal care (that is, with eating, getting out of bed or a chair, dressing, bathing and using the toilet)?	01	02	-1
c.	by fixing meals or preparing special foods for (him/her)?	01	02	-1
d.	by doing (his/her) laundry, by going shopping for (him/her) or doing day-to-day housework (around (his/her) home)?	01	02	-1
e.	by doing chores (like washing windows or making minor repairs) (around (his/her) home)?	01	02	-1
f.	by driving (him/her) places or helping (him/her) use public transportation?	01	02	-1
g.	by helping manage (his/her) money (for example, writing checks or paying bills)?	01	02	-1
		CONTINUE WITH B7, NEXT PAGE		

REGULARLY = ON A ROUTINE BASIS WITH
HELP PROVIDED AT LEAST ONCE A MONTH.

NAME 2 _____   NAME 3 _____   NAME 4 _____

YES	NO	NA	YES	NO	NA	YES	NO	NA
01	02	-1	01	02	-1	01	02	-1
01	02	-1	01	02	-1	01	02	-1
01	02	-1	01	02	-1	01	02	-1
01	02	-1	01	02	-1	01	02	-1
01	02	-1	01	02	-1	01	02	-1
01	02	-1	01	02	-1	01	02	-1
01	02	-1	01	02	-1	01	02	-1

CONTINUE WITH B7, NEXT PAGE.　　　CONTINUE WITH B7, NEXT PAGE.　　　CONTINUE WITH B7, NEXT PAGE.

- 23 -

NAME 1 _____

B7. INTERVIEWER: (CAN/COULD) <u>SAMPLE MEMBER</u> BE LEFT ALONE? (IS A20 CODED "YES"?)	YES . . . . 01 (B9) NO. . . . . 02 A20 NOT ANSWERED. . . 03
B8. (Does/Did) <u>NAME</u> regularly help by staying there because <u>SAMPLE MEMBER</u> (cannot/could not) be left alone?	YES . . . . 01 NO. . . . . 02 NA. . . . . -1
B9. (Does/Did) <u>NAME</u> regularly spend time just keeping <u>SAMPLE MEMBER</u> company, for example, by sitting and talking or watching TV?	YES . . . . 01 NO. . . . . 02 NA. . . . . -1

B10. Thinking about all the things that <u>NAME</u> (does/did) to help <u>SAMPLE MEMBER</u>, about how many hours would you say <u>NAME</u> (spends/spent) helping (him/her) on an average day?
 	
PROBE: On an average day when (he/she) (helps/helped)?
 	
Your best estimate will be fine.
	|___|___|.|___| HOURS
	  A DAY
	NA. . . . . -1
	
	DECIMAL FRACTIONS OF AN HOUR:
	5 MINUTES
	  OR LESS = 00.1 HOURS
	10 MINUTES = 00.2 HOURS
	15 MINUTES = 00.2 HOURS
	20 MINUTES = 00.3 HOURS
	25 MINUTES = 00.4 HOURS
	30 MINUTES = 00.5 HOURS
	35 MINUTES = 00.6 HOURS
	45 MINUTES = 00.8 HOURS
	50 MINUTES = 00.8 HOURS
	55 MINUTES = 00.9 HOURS

B11. INTERVIEWER: WAS ANOTHER CAREGIVER NAMED IN B1?	YES . (REPEAT B2-B11) 01 NO. . (GO TO B12) . . 02

REGULARLY = ON A ROUTINE BASIS WITH HELP
PROVIDED AT LEAST ONCE A MONTH.

NAME 2 _____   NAME 3 _____   NAME 4 _____

YES 01 (B9)	YES 01 (B9)	YES 01 (B9)
NO. 02	NO. 02	NO. 02
A20 NOT ANSWERED . . 03	A20 NOT ANSWERED . . 03	A20 NOT ANSWERED . . 03
YES 01	YES 01	YES 01
NO. 02	NO. 02	NO. 02
NA. . . . . −1	NA. . . . . −1	NA. . . . . −1
YES 01	YES 01	YES 01
NO. 02	NO. 02	NO. 02
NA. . . . . −1	NA. . . . . −1	NA. . . . . −1
|__|__|.|__| HOURS A DAY NA. . . . . . . −1	|__|__|.|__| HOURS A DAY NA. . . . . . . −1	|__|__|.|__| HOURS A DAY NA. . . . . . . −1
DECIMAL FRACTIONS OF AN HOUR: 5 MINUTES OR LESS = 00.1 HOURS 10 MINUTES = 00.2 HOURS 15 MINUTES = 00.2 HOURS 20 MINUTES = 00.3 HOURS 25 MINUTES = 00.4 HOURS 30 MINUTES = 00.5 HOURS 35 MINUTES = 00.6 HOURS 45 MINUTES = 00.8 HOURS 50 MINUTES = 00.8 HOURS 55 MINUTES = 00.9 HOURS	DECIMAL FRACTIONS OF AN HOUR: 5 MINUTES OR LESS = 00.1 HOURS 10 MINUTES = 00.2 HOURS 15 MINUTES = 00.2 HOURS 20 MINUTES = 00.3 HOURS 25 MINUTES = 00.4 HOURS 30 MINUTES = 00.5 HOURS 35 MINUTES = 00.6 HOURS 45 MINUTES = 00.8 HOURS 50 MINUTES = 00.8 HOURS 55 MINUTES = 00.9 HOURS	DECIMAL FRACTIONS OF AN HOUR: 5 MINUTES OR LESS = 00.1 HOURS 10 MINUTES = 00.2 HOURS 15 MINUTES = 00.2 HOURS 20 MINUTES = 00.3 HOURS 25 MINUTES = 00.4 HOURS 30 MINUTES = 00.5 HOURS 35 MINUTES = 00.6 HOURS 45 MINUTES = 00.8 HOURS 50 MINUTES = 00.8 HOURS 55 MINUTES = 00.9 HOURS
YES.(REPEAT B2–B11). . 01 NO . . (GO TO B12) . . 02	YES.(REPEAT B2–B11). . 01 NO . . (GO TO B12) . . 02	(GO TO B12)

B12. Now, please think about all of <u>SAMPLE MEMBER'S</u> friends and family members <u>and</u> people who may help (him/her) as part of their paid or volunteer work.

If you (were/had been) unable to help <u>SAMPLE MEMBER</u>, (is/was) there someone who would (do/have done) the things that you (do/did)?

```
YES . . . . . . . . . . . . . . . 01
NO  . . . . . . . . . . . . . . . 02 (B16)
NOT ANSWERED. . . . . . . . . . . -1 (B16)
```

B13. Who (is/was) that?

PROBE IF MORE THAN ONE NAMED: Who would be most likely to do it or to help the most?

RECORD FIRST NAME OR TITLE ONLY.

NAME/TITLE _____

B14. INTERVIEWER: IS PERSON NAMED IN B13 --

SOMEONE NAMED IN B1. . . . . 01 ⟶ ⎰ GRID LOCATION
                                            ⎱ B.01.|___| (B16)

NOT NAMED. 02

B15. CODE WITHOUT ASKING IF KNOWN.

Is <u>NAME FROM B13</u> related to <u>SAMPLE MEMBER</u>?

IF YES: How?

IF NO: Is (he/she) a friend or an employee?

```
SPOUSE . . . . . . . . . . . . . . . . . . 01
DAUGHTER . . . . . . . . . . . . . . . . . 02
SON. . . . . . . . . . . . . . . . . . . . 03
SISTER . . . . . . . . . . . . . . . . . . 04
BROTHER. . . . . . . . . . . . . . . . . . 05
PARENT . . . . . . . . . . . . . . . . . . 06
DAUGHTER-IN-LAW. . . . . . . . . . . . . . 07
SON-IN-LAW . . . . . . . . . . . . . . . . 08
SISTER-IN-LAW. . . . . . . . . . . . . . . 09
BROTHER-IN-LAW . . . . . . . . . . . . . . 10
GRANDCHILD . . . . . . . . . . . . . . . . 11
OTHER RELATIVE . . . . . . . . . . . . . . 12
FRIEND OR NEIGHBOR . . . . . . . . . . . . 13
EMPLOYEE OF SAMPLE MEMBER. . . . . . . . . 14
EMPLOYEE OR VOLUNTEER FROM ORGANIZATION. 15
NOT ANSWERED . . . . . . . . . . . . . . . -1
```

B16. INTERVIEWER: IS SAMPLE MEMBER CURRENTLY IN A NURSING HOME?
      (IS S3 CODED "03"?)

                          YES. 01 (B20)

                          NO 02

                          S3 NOT ANSWERED. 03

B17. All things considered, how likely do you think it is that <u>SAMPLE MEMBER</u>
      will be placed in a nursing home in the next year? Would you say (he/she)
      probably will, that there is an even chance, or that (he/she) probably will
      not?

                          PROBABLY WILL. 01

                          EVEN CHANCE. 02 (B20)

                          PROBABLY WILL NOT. . . . 03 (B19)

                          NOT ANSWERED . . . . . . -1 (B20)

B18. Are you pretty certain that (he/she) will?

                          YES. 01

                          NO 02

                          NOT ANSWERED . . . . . -1

                    *** ALL SKIP TO B20.***

B19. Are you pretty certain that (he/she) will not?

                          YES. 01

                          NO 02

                          NOT ANSWERED . . . . . -1

B20. INTERVIEWER: IS THE RESPONDENT THE SPOUSE OF THE SAMPLE MEMBER?
      (IS S1 CODED "01"?)   YES. 01 (C4)

                               NO 02

                               S1 NOT ANSWERED. 03

C. EXPENDITURES

C1. Now I would like to ask about any extra financial costs you may have
because of SAMPLE MEMBER'S disability. Sometimes helping to take care of
someone who is ill or disabled costs extra money that is not paid back or
reimbursed by insurance.

In the last (month/month when you were helping regularly) did you spend any
extra money, that you will not be paid back --

REGULARLY = ON A ROUTINE BASIS WITH HELP PROVIDED
AT LEAST ONCE A MONTH.

		IF YES ─────────➤		
		YES	NO	NA
a. for medical bills, nursing home bills, prescription medicines or special equipment?		01	02	-1

  PROBE: Special equipment like a walker or
         raised toilet seat?

  EXCLUDE VISITING NURSES AND THERAPISTS.

| b. for care or services for (him/her), for example, for a home health aide, home-delivered meals? . . . . | | 01 | 02 | -1 |

| c. for (his/her) housing, that is, for rent or mortgage payments, utilities, including heat, and maintenance?. . . . . | | 01 | 02 | -1 |

  EXCLUDE TELEPHONE.

| d. for food or clothing for (him/her)?. . . . . | | 01 | 02 | -1 |

| e. in (the last/that) month, did you give (him/her) spending money? . . . . | | 01 | 02 | -1 |

  PROBE; That is, money for no specific bill?

| f. anything else? SPECIFY_____ . . . . | | 01 | 02 | -1 |

_____

QC ONLY

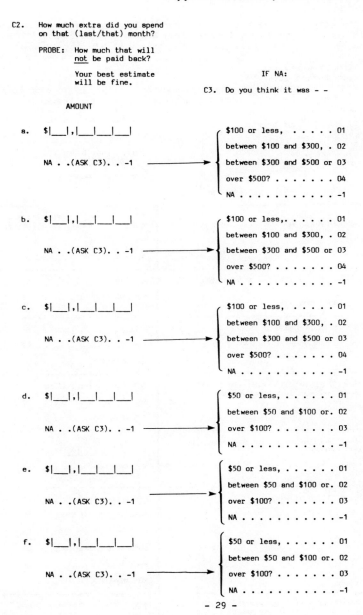

C2.   How much extra did you spend
on that (last/that) month?

    PROBE: How much that will
__not__ be paid back?

              Your best estimate
will be fine.

AMOUNT

IF NA:

C3.   Do you think it was - -

a. $|__|,|__|__|__|

NA . .(ASK C3). . -1 ⟶

$100 or less, ... 01

between $100 and $300, . 02

between $300 and $500 or 03

over $500? 04

NA . . . . -1

b. $|__|,|__|__|__|

NA . .(ASK C3). . -1 ⟶

$100 or less,. 01

between $100 and $300, . 02

between $300 and $500 or 03

over $500? 04

NA . . . . -1

c. $|__|,|__|__|__|

NA . .(ASK C3). . -1 ⟶

$100 or less, ... 01

between $100 and $300, . 02

between $300 and $500 or 03

over $500? 04

NA . . . . -1

d. $|__|,|__|__|__|

NA . .(ASK C3). . -1 ⟶

$50 or less, ... 01

between $50 and $100 or. 02

over $100? 03

NA . . . . -1

e. $|__|,|__|__|__|

NA . .(ASK C3). . -1 ⟶

$50 or less, ... 01

between $50 and $100 or. 02

over $100? 03

NA . . . . -1

f. $|__|,|__|__|__|

NA . .(ASK C3). . -1 ⟶

$50 or less, ... 01

between $50 and $100 or. 02

over $100? 03

NA . . . . -1

C4. In the last (month,/month when you were helping regularly), did other relatives or friends spend extra money taking care of SAMPLE MEMBER because of (his/her) disability, that they will not be paid back?

    IF YES: Who was that?
    PROBE: Anyone else?
    IF MORE THAN 4 NAMED: I have some questions about the four of these who contributed the most. Who are they?

REGULARLY = ON A
ROUTINE BASIS WITH
HELP PROVIDED AT LEAST
ONCE A MONTH.

RECORD FIRST NAME ONLY.

NAME 1 _____

DON'T KNOW IF OTHERS
   CONTRIBUTE . . . . -1 (C12)

NO OTHER FINANCIAL
   CAREGIVERS . . . . -4 (C12)

ASK C5-C11 FOR EACH FINANCIAL CAREGIVER

C5. INTERVIEWER: WAS NAME ALSO NAMED IN B1?	GRID LOCATION YES . . . . 01 ➤ B-01-|___| (C9) NO . . . . 02 B1 NA . . . 03
C6. How is NAME related to SAMPLE MEMBER? SEE CODES OPPOSITE.	RELATIONSHIP . . . |___|___| NOT ANSWERED. . . . . . . -1
C7. CODE WITHOUT ASKING IF KNOWN: And is NAME male or female?	MALE. . . . . 01 FEMALE. . . . . 02 NOT ANSWERED. . . . . . . -1
C8. (Does/Did) NAME live with SAMPLE MEMBER (when you were last helping regularly)?	YES . . . . 01 NO. . . . . 02 NOT ANSWERED. . . . . . . -1
C9. About how much extra did NAME spend (last/that) month? PROBE: Your best estimate will be fine.	$|___|,|___|___|___| (C11) NOT ANSWERED. . . . . . . -1
C10. Do you think it was --	$50 or less,. . . . . . . 01 between $50 and $100, . . 02 between $100 and $300, . 03 between $300 and $500, . 04 over $500? . . . . 05 NOT ANSWERED. . . . . . . -1
C11. INTERVIEWER: WAS ANOTHER FINANCIAL CAREGIVER NAMED?	YES . (REPEAT C5-11). . . 01 NO. . (GO TO C12) 02

```
                          RELATIONSHIP CODES
     SPOUSE . . . . . . . .  01      SON-IN-LAW . . . . . . .  08

     DAUGHTER . . . . . . .  02      SISTER-IN-LAW. . . . .  09

     SON. . . . . . . . . .  03      BROTHER-IN-LAW . . . .  10

     SISTER . . . . . . . .  04      GRANDCHILD . . . . . .  11

     BROTHER. . . . . . . .  05      OTHER RELATIVE . . . .  12

     PARENT . . . . . . . .  06      FRIEND OR NEIGHBOR . . .  13

     DAUGHTER-IN-LAW . . . .  07

                CODES 14 AND 15 ARE NOT APPLICABLE
```

NAME 2 _____   NAME 3 _____   NAME 4 _____

YES . . . . 01 → GRID LOCATION B-01-|___|(C9) NO . . . . 02 B1 NA . . . 03	YES . . . . 01 → GRID LOCATION B-01-|___|(C9) NO . . . . 02 B1 NA . . . 03	YES . . . . 01 → GRID LOCATION B-01-|___|(C9) NO . . . . 02 B1 NA . . . 03
RELATIONSHIP . . . |__|__| NOT ANSWERED. . . . . . . -1	RELATIONSHIP . . . |__|__| NOT ANSWERED. . . . . . . -1	RELATIONSHIP . . . |__|__| NOT ANSWERED. . . . . . . -1
MALE. . . . . 01 FEMALE. . . . . 02 NOT ANSWERED. . . . . . . -1	MALE. . . . . 01 FEMALE. . . . . 02 NOT ANSWERED. . . . . . . -1	MALE. . . . . 01 FEMALE. . . . . 02 NOT ANSWERED. . . . . . . -1
YES . . . . 01 NO. . . . . 02 NOT ANSWERED. . . . . . . -1	YES . . . . 01 NO. . . . . 02 NOT ANSWERED. . . . . . . -1	YES . . . . 01 NO. . . . . 02 NOT ANSWERED. . . . . . . -1
$|__|,|__|__|__| (C11) NOT ANSWERED. . . . . . . -1	$|__|,|__|__|__| (C11) NOT ANSWERED. . . . . . . -1	$|__|,|__|__|__| (C11) NOT ANSWERED. . . . . . . -1
$50 or less, ... 01 between $50 and $100, . . 02 between $100 and $300, . 03 between $300 and $500, . 04 over $500? . . . . . . 05 NOT ANSWERED. . . . . . . -1	$50 or less, ... 01 between $50 and $100, . . 02 between $100 and $300, . 03 between $300 and $500, . 04 over $500? . . . . . . 05 NOT ANSWERED. . . . . . . -1	$50 or less, ... 01 between $50 and $100, . . 02 between $100 and $300, . 03 between $300 and $500, . 04 over $500? . . . . . . 05 NOT ANSWERED. . . . . . . -1
YES . (REPEAT C5-11). . . 01 NO. . (GO TO C12) 02	YES . (REPEAT C5-11). . . 01 NO. . (GO TO C12) 02	GO TO C12.

C12. INTERVIEWER: IS THE RESPONDENT THE SPOUSE OF THE SAMPLE MEMBER/
     (IS S1 CODED "01"?)

                            YES. 01 (D1)

                            NO 02

                            S1 NOT ANSWERED. 03

C13. Sometimes people who are disabled help out with the expenses others have to
     take care of them.

     Thinking about just yourself, in the last (month/month when you were
     helping regularly), did <u>you</u> have expenses because of taking care of <u>SAMPLE
     MEMBER</u> that (he/she) helped to pay or reimbursed you for?

     PROBE: For example, for   YES 01
             gas for your car
             (to visit (him/her)/   NO. 02
             take (him/her) places)?
                                     DON'T KNOW. . . . . -1

D. STRESS AND BEHAVIOR

D1. Next I'd like to ask you some questions about your attitudes and feelings.

In general, how satisfying do you find the way you're spending your life these days? Would you call it completely satisfying, pretty satisfying or not very satisfying?

COMPLETELY SATISFYING	01
PRETTY SATISFYING	02
NOT VERY SATISFYING	03
NOT ANSWERED	-1

D2. People who help others sometimes worry about obtaining sufficient help or assistance for them. Would you say you worry about that quite a lot, sometimes, rarely, or not at all?

QUITE A LOT	01
SOMETIMES	02
RARELY	03
NOT AT ALL	04
NOT ANSWERED	-1

D3. The arrangements to care for someone may involve services like meals on wheels and help from people as part of their paid or volunteer work, as well as help from friends and family.

Please think about all of the arrangements to care for SAMPLE MEMBER (when you were last helping regularly). In general how satisfied (are/were) you with these arrangements? Would you say --

REGULARLY = ON A
ROUTINE BASIS WITH
HELP PROVIDED AT LEAST
ONCE A MONTH.

very satisfied, ...	01
somewhat satisfied, or.	02
not too satisfied.	03
NO OTHER ARRANGEMENTS	04
NOT ANSWERED	-1

D4. We would like to get some idea of the amount of stress or strain that caring for <u>SAMPLE MEMBER</u> (places/placed) on you.

   I'm going to mention several areas in which a person might experience stress or strain. By choosing a number from 1 to 5, please tell me how much strain you experience(d). The <u>greater</u> the strain, the <u>higher</u> the number you should choose.

   PROBE: (At the present time/When you were last helping regularly)?

	LITTLE OR NO				GREAT DEAL	NA
a. First, <u>emotional</u> strain. Please choose a number from 1 to 5 where 1 means you experience(d) little or no emotional strain and 5 means a great deal of emotional strain.	01	02	03	04	05	-1
b. What about <u>physical</u> strain?	01	02	03	04	05	-1

   PROBE: Choose a number from 1 to 5, where 1 means little or no strain and 5 means a great deal of strain.

   PROBE: For example, from heavy work like lifting (him/her) or fatigue from caring for (him/her) for long periods?

c. And <u>financial</u> strain?	01	02	03	04	05	-1

   PROBE: Choose a number from 1 to 5, where 1 means little or no strain and 5 means a great deal of strain.

D5. Sometimes a disabled older person's behavior can be a problem. Please tell me if you (have/had) any of the following problems with <u>SAMPLE MEMBER</u>.

   PROBE: In the last month (you were helping regularly)?

	<u>YES</u>	<u>NO</u>	<u>NA</u>
a. (Does/Did) (he/she) sometimes become upset and yell at you or refuse to cooperate?	01	02	-1
b. (Does/Did) (he/she) embarrass you or others?.	01	02	-1
c. (Does/Did) (he/she) forget things, or get confused?.	01	02 (D7)	-1 (D7)

D6. IF D5c IS "YES":

(Is/Was) that a serious problem for you or not?

YES, SERIOUS 01

NO, NOT SERIOUS. 02

NOT ANSWERED . . . .-1

D7. INTERVIEWER: (DOES/DID) RESPONDENT LIVE WITH SAMPLE MEMBER?
(IS A1 CODED "01"?)

YES. 01

NO 02 (D10)

A1 NOT ANSWERED. 03 (D10)

D8. (Is/Was) your sleep ever interrupted because you (have/had) to get up to
take care of SAMPLE MEMBER?

PROBE: In the last month   YES. 01
(you were helping
regularly)?   NO 02 (D10)

NOT ANSWERED . . . .-1 (D10)

D9. About how many times in an average week (is/was) your sleep interrupted
because you (have/had) to get up to take care of SAMPLE MEMBER?

TIMES PER WEEK . . . . . . |___|___|

LESS THAN ONCE A WEEK. 00

NOT ANSWERED . . . .-1

D10. Now, I'm going to read a list of problems people sometimes have when taking care of a disabled person. For each one, please tell me whether it (is/was) <u>true</u> for you or <u>not</u>.

PROBE: (At the present time/when you were last helping regularly)?　　IF TRUE ⟶ D11. (Is/Was) that a serious problem for you or not?

	TRUE	NOT TRUE	NA	YES, SERIOUS	NO, NOT SERIOUS	NA
a. Taking care of <u>SAMPLE MEMBER</u> limits the time you have to spend with (your children or) other family members Is this true for you or not? . . .	01	02	-1	01	02	-1
b. You do not have as much privacy when you take care of (him/her). .	01	02	-1	01	02	-1
c. Taking care of (him/her) limits your social life or free time . .	01	02	-1	01	02	-1
d. You have to give (him/her) almost constant attention	01	02	-1	01	02	-1
e. Taking care of (him/her) is hard on your relationships with those you are close to (such as your (husband/wife/children))	01	02	-1	01	02	-1

D12. In general, how well (do/did) you and <u>SAMPLE MEMBER</u> get along (when you were last helping regularly)? Would you say that you (get/got) along <u>very</u> well, (<u>fairly/pretty</u>) well, or not too well?

VERY WELL 01

FAIRLY WELL 02

NOT TOO WELL 03

NOT ANSWERED . . . . -1

REGULARY = ON A ROUTINE BASIS WITH HELP PROVIDED AT LEAST ONCE A MONTH.

E. DEMOGRAPHIC AND EMPLOYMENT INFORMATION

E1. We are interested in knowing more about the kinds of people who give care. The last questions are about you.

What is your date of birth?

|___|___| |___|___| |___|___|___|___|
  MONTH   DAY   YEAR

NOT ANSWERED . . . . -1

E2. What is the highest grade or year you finished in school?

IF UNGRADED OR FOREIGN SCHOOL: About what grade would that be equal to (in this country)?

NO SCHOOLING 00

ELEMENTARY (1-8) . . . . .|___|___|

SECONDARY (9-12) . . . . .|___|___|

COLLEGE/GRADUATE/OTHER
  POST SECONDARY . . . . .|___|___|

NOT ANSWERED . . . . -1

E3. CODE WITHOUT ASKING IF KNOWN (SEE S1).
And are you --

male, or 01

female? 02

NOT ANSWERED . . . . -1

E4. What is your racial or ethnic background?
READ CATEGORIES IF NECESSARY.

PROBE: Are you of Spanish origin?

IF IN-PERSON, ASK IF NOT OBVIOUS.

AMERICAN INDIAN/ALASKAN NATIVE . 01

ASIAN/PACIFIC ISLANDER 02

BLACK, NOT OF HISPANIC ORIGIN. . 03

HISPANIC 04

WHITE, NOT OF HISPANIC ORIGIN. . 05

NOT ANSWERED . . . . -1

E5. CODE WITHOUT ASKING IF KNOWN (SEE S1).
     Are you <u>now</u> married, widowed, divorced or separated, or have you never been
     married?

                                        MARRIED 01

                                        WIDOWED 02

                                        DIVORCED 03

                                        SEPARATED. 04

                                        NEVER MARRIED 05

                                        NOT ANSWERED . . . . -1

E6. CODE WITHOUT ASKING IF KNOWN.
     Does anyone (else) now live or stay with <u>you</u> (apart from <u>SAMPLE MEMBER</u>)?

                                        YES 01

                                        NO 02 (E8)

                                        NOT ANSWERED . . . . -1 (E8)

E7. Do you have any children under fifteen living with you?

                    IF YES ⟶ How many? . . . . |___|___|

     PROBE: At the present   NO/NONE. 00
             time?
                               NOT ANSWERED . . . . -1

E8. The next few questions are about <u>your</u> health. Since we're talking with a
     wide variety of people, some of the questions may not seem to apply to
     you. Even so, it's important that we have complete answers from everyone.

     Compared to other people your own age, would you say that your health in
     general is --

     PROBE: At the present   excellent, ... 01
             time?
                               good,. 02

                               fair, or 03

                               poor?. 04

                               NOT ANSWERED . . . . -1

E9.   Because of health or disability, do <u>you</u> have any problem preparing meals,
      doing housework, laundry, or shopping, taking medicine, traveling out of
      walking distance, managing your money, or using the telephone?

      PROBE: At the present   YES, PROBLEM WITH AT LEAST ONE . 01
              time?

                            NO PROBLEM 02

                            NOT ANSWERED . . . . -1

E10. Because of health or disability, do <u>you</u> have any problem eating, getting
      out of bed or a chair, dressing, bathing, or using the toilet?

      PROBE: At the present   YES, PROBLEM WITH AT LEAST ONE . 01
              time?

                            NO PROBLEM 02

                            NOT ANSWERED . . . . -1

E11. Now, I have some questions about employment. Are you <u>currently</u> working
      for pay at a job or business?

                            YES 01

                            NO 02 (E17)

                            NOT ANSWERED . . . . -1 (E17)

E12. How many hours per week do you usually work?

                            HOURS PER WEEK . .|___|___|

                            NOT ANSWERED . . . . -1 (E14)

E13. INTERVIEWER: DOES RESPONDENT WORK <u>FEWER</u> THAN 35 HOURS PER WEEK?
      (SEE E12.)

                            YES 01

                            NO   . . . . 02(E15)

                            E12 NOT ANSWERED 03

E14. Are you working <u>fewer</u> hours now than you would like to because of taking care of <u>SAMPLE MEMBER</u>?

                                     YES 01

                                     NO 02

                                     NOT ANSWERED . . . . -1

E15. To better understand the employment of people who give care, we would like some information about your earnings.

      Please estimate how much you earn in an average week or month, <u>before</u> taxes and other deductions, but including overtime pay, tips, bonuses and commissions.

                                                          ⎧ PER WEEK . . 01 (E18)
      EARNINGS. . . $|___|___|___| , |___|___|___| ⟶ ⎨ PER MONTH. . 02 (E18)
                                                          ⎩ PER YEAR . . 03 (E18)

          PROBE: For an average   DON'T KNOW . . . . -1
                  week or month
                  at the present   REFUSED. . . . . -3
                  time?

      IF SELF-EMPLOYED, GET AVERAGE
      NET MONTHLY INCOME FROM
      BUSINESS OR FARM.

E16. Well, would you say it was <u>more</u> than $400 a month or <u>less</u> than $400 a month?

                                     MORE THAN $400 01

                                     LESS THAN $400 02

                                     EXACTLY $400 03

                                     DON'T KNOW . . . . -1

                                     REFUSED. . . . . -3

┌───┐
│   *** ALL SKIP TO E18. ***   │
└───┘

E17. Have you worked at a job for pay within the past year?

                          YES 01

                          NO 02 (E19)

                          NOT ANSWERED . . . . -1 (E19)

E18. Sometimes taking care of someone can affect your work on a job. I'm
      going to read some ways this may happen. Please tell me whether these
      things have happened to you in the past year because you had to take care
      of SAMPLE MEMBER.

                                                YES   NO   NA

       a. First, in the past year have you
          had to turn down a job or refuse
          a more responsible position
          because you were taking care
          of (him/her)? 01   02   -1

       b. Have you had to leave a job?. 01   02   -1

          PROBE: In the past year because
                  you were taking care of
                  (him/her)?

       c. Have you been unable to look
          for (a/another) job when you
          wanted to? 01   02   -1

          PROBE: At anytime in the past year
                  because you were taking care
                  of (him/her)?

┌───┐
│   *** ALL SKIP TO E22. ***   │
└───┘

┌──┐
│ E19.│ INTERVIEWER: IS RESPONDENT UNDER 70? (SEE E1.)   │
│   │   │
│   │   YES, UNDER 70. 01   │
│   │   │
│   │   NO, 70 OR MORE . . . . . 02 (E24)   │
│   │   │
│   │   E1 NOT ANSWERED. 03   │
└──┘

E20. Have you had to turn down a job <u>in the past year</u> because you were taking care of <u>SAMPLE MEMBER</u>?

                         YES 01

                         NO 02

                         NOT ANSWERED . . . . -1

E21. In the past year, have you been unable to look for work when you wanted to because you were caring for (him/her)?

                         YES 01

                         NO 02

                         NOT ANSWERED . . . . -1

```
+-----------------------------------------------------------------+
|                     *** ALL SKIP TO E24. ***                    |
+-----------------------------------------------------------------+
```

```
+-----+-----------------------------------------------------------+
|E22. | INTERVIEWER:  IS RESPONDENT CURRENTLY WORKING FEWER HOURS  |
|     | THAN HE/SHE WOULD LIKE BECAUSE OF CARING FOR SAMPLE MEMBER?|
|     | (IS E14 ANSWERED "YES"?)                                  |
|     |                   YES . . . . . . . . . . 01 (E24)        |
|     |                   NO  . . . . . . . . . . 02              |
|     |                   E14 NOT ANSWERED . . . . . 03           |
+-----+-----------------------------------------------------------+
```

E23. CODE WITHOUT ASKING IF KNOWN.

(Even though it's not true now, at anytime in/In) the past year, have you had to work fewer hours than you would like because you were taking care of (him/her)?

                         YES 01

                         NO 02

                         NOT ANSWERED . . . . -1

E24. Finally, we are trying to get some idea of the income range of people who give care.

Last month <u>before</u> taxes and other deductions, was (your total income/the total combined income for you and all members of your household) <u>more</u> than $1,000 or <u>less</u> than $1,000? Include money from jobs, net income from a business or farm, dividends, interest, net income from rent, Social Security payments, and all other money income received by you and your household. Was it --

more than $1,000,. 01 (E26)

less than $1,000, or 02

exactly $1,000?. 03 (E27)

DON'T KNOW . . . . -1 (E27)

REFUSED. . . . . -3 (E27)

E25. Was it --

READ UNTIL RESPONDENT
IDENTIFIES CATEGORY.

$300 or less, ... 01

between $300 and $500, ... 02

between $500 and $800, or. . . . 03

between $800 and $999? 04

DON'T KNOW . . . . -1

REFUSED. . . . . -3

*** ALL SKIP TO E27. ***

E26. Was it --

READ UNTIL RESPONDENT   between $1,000 and $1,500, . . . 01
IDENTIFIES CATEGORY.
                                     between $1,500 and $2,000, . . . 02

                                     between $2,000 and $3,000, . . . 03

                                     between $3,000 and $4,000, or. . 04

                                     over $4,000? 05

                                     DON'T KNOW . . . . -1

                                     REFUSED. . . . . -3

E27. Thank you. This concludes our questions; in six months we would like to
      (call/come back) to see how you are getting on. Could you please tell me
      the name, address, and phone number of someone we might contact in case we
      have trouble getting in touch with you?

      RECORD AT CONTACT SHEET 14.

      Thank you very much for your time.

```
    *** ALL SKIP TO E29. ***
```

E28. Our survey is of friends and family members who regularly help take care of
      someone now or who have done so quite recently. Thank you very much for
      your time in answering my questions.

```
  E29.                                 AM . . . 01
              END TIME:  |___|___|:|___|___|
                                       PM . . . 02
```

Bibliography

Anderson, Nancy, Sharon Patten, and Jay Greenberg. *A Comparison of Home Care and Nursing Home Care for Older Persons in Minnesota.* Minneapolis: Hubert H. Humphrey Institute of Public Affairs and Center for Health Services Research, University of Minnesota, 1980.

Arling, Greg, and William J. McAuley. "The Feasibility of Public Payments for Family Caregiving." *The Gerontologist,* vol. 23, 1983, pp. 300–306.

Baxter, Raymond J., Robert Applebaum, James J. Callahan, Jr., Jon B. Christianson, and Stephen L. Day. *The Planning and Implementation of Channeling: Early Experiences of the National Long Term Care Demonstration.* Princeton, N.J.: Mathematica Policy Research, Inc., April 16, 1983.

Branch, Laurence G., and Alan M. Jette. "Elders' Use of Informal Long-Term Care Assistance." *The Gerontologist,* vol. 23, 1983, pp. 51–56.

Brody, Elaine M. "Parent Care as a Normative Family Stress." *The Gerontologist,* vol. 25, 1985, pp. 19–29.

———. "Women in the Middle and Family Help to Older People." *The Gerontologist,* vol. 21, 1981, pp. 471–480.

———. "Women's Changing Roles, The Aging Family and Long Term Care of Older People." *National Journal,* vol. 11, 1979, pp. 1828–1833.

Brody, Stanley J., S. Walter Poulshock, and Carla F. Masciocchi. "The Family Caring Unit: A Major Consideration in the Long-Term Support System." *The Gerontologist,* vol. 18, 1978, pp. 556–561.

Callahan, James J., Lawrence D. Diamond, Janet Z. Giele, and Robert Morris. "Responsibility of Families for Their Severely Disabled Elders." *Health Care Financing Review,* vol. 1, 1980, pp. 29–48.

Campbell, Angus, Phillip E. Converse, and Willard L. Rodgers. *The Quality of American Life: Perceptions, Evaluation, and Satisfactions.* New York, N.Y.: Russell Sage Foundation, 1976.

Cantor, Marjorie H. "Strain Among Caregivers: A Study of Experience in the United States." *The Gerontologist,* vol. 23, 1983, pp. 597–604.

———. "Caring for the Frail Elderly: Impact on Family, Friends, and Neighbors." Paper presented at the 33rd Annual Meeting of the Gerontological Society of America, San Diego, Calif., November 1980.

———. Collateral Questionnaire for the study, "The Impact of the Entry of the

Formal Organization on the Existing Informal Networks of Older Americans," Fordham University's Center on Gerontology, April 1979.

————. "Neighbors and Friends: An Overlooked Resource in the Informal Support System." Paper presented at the 30th Annual Meeting of the Gerontological Society, San Francisco, Calif., 1977.

Caro, Francis G., and Arthur Blank. *Home Care in New York City: The System, The Providers, The Beneficiaries.* New York, N.Y.: Community Service Society, 1985.

————. "Burden Experienced by Informal Providers of Home Care for the Elderly." Paper presented at the Annual Meeting of the Gerontological Society, San Antonio, Texas, November 1984.

Cerf, Joanna, Audrey McDonald, and Barbara Phillips. *National Long Term Care Demonstration Caregiver Baseline Instrument Training Manual.* Princeton, N.J.: Mathematica Policy Research, Inc., November 1982.

Christianson, Jon B. *Plan for the Analysis of Impacts on Channeling on Informal Caregiving and Caregivers.* Princeton, N.J.: Mathematica Policy Research, Inc., June 30, 1983.

Christianson, Jon B., and Susan A. Stephens. *Informal Care to the Impaired Elderly: Report of the National Long Term Care Demonstration Survey of Informal Caregivers.* Princeton, N.J.: Mathematica Policy Research, Inc., June 1984.

Cicirelli, Victor G. *Helping Elderly Parents—The Role of Adult Children.* Boston, Mass.: Auburn House, 1981.

Clark, Robert L., and John A. Menefee. "Federal Expenditures for the Elderly: Past and Future." *The Gerontologist,* vol. 21, 1981, pp. 132–137.

Congressional Budget Office. *Long Term Care for the Elderly and Disabled.* Budget Issue Paper, Washington, D.C., February 1977.

Demkovich, Linda E. "In Treating the Problems of the Elderly There May Be No Place Like Home." *National Journal,* vol. 11, 1979, pp. 2154–2158.

Dunlop, Burton D. "Expanded Home-Based Care for the Impaired Elderly: Solution or Pipe Dream?" *American Journal of Public Health,* vol. 70, 1980, pp. 514–518.

Fengler, Alfred P., and Nancy Goodrich. "Wives of Elderly Disabled Men: The Hidden Patients." *The Gerontologist,* vol. 19, 1979, pp. 175–185.

Frankfather, Dwight L., Michael J. Smith, and Francis G. Caro. *Family Care of the Elderly.* Cambridge, Mass.: Lexington Books, 1981.

General Accounting Office. *The Well-Being of Older People in Cleveland, Ohio.* HRD-77-70, Washington, D.C., April 19, 1977.

Greenberg, Jay N., D. Doth, A.N. Johnson, and C. Austin. *A Comparative Study of Long Term Care Demonstration Projects: Lessons for Future Inquiry.* Minneapolis, Minn.: Center for the Health Services Research, University of Minnesota, 1980.

Greene, Vernon L. "Substitution between Formally and Informally Provided Care for the Impaired Elderly in the Community." *Medical Care,* vol. 21, 1983, pp. 609–619.

Gross-Andrew, Susannah, and Anna H. Zimmer. "Incentives to Families Caring for Disabled Elderly: Research and Demonstration Project to Strengthen the Natural Support System." *Journal of Gerontological Social Work,* vol. 1, 1978, pp. 119–133.

Gurland, Barry, Laura Dean, Roni Gurland, and Diana Cook. "Personal Time Dependency in the Elderly of New York City: Findings from the U.S.–U.K. Cross National Geriatric Community Study." In Community Council of Greater New York, *Dependency of the Elderly of New York City: Report of a Research Utilization Workshop*. New York, N.Y., October 1978.

Health Care Financing Administration. *Long Term Care: Background and Future Directions*. Discussion Paper HCFA 81-20047, Washington, D.C., January 1981.

Hooyman, Nancy, Judith Gonea, and Rhonda Montgomery. "The Impact of In-Home Services Termination on Family Caregivers." *The Gerontologist*, vol. 25, 1985, pp. 141–145.

Horowitz, Amy. "Sons and Daughters as Caregivers to Older Parents: Differences in Role Performance and Consequences." Paper presented at the Annual Scientific Meeting of the Gerontological Society of America, Toronto, Canada, November 1981.

———. "Families Who Care: A Study of Natural Support Systems of the Elderly." Paper presented at the 31st Scientific Meeting of the Gerontological Society, Dallas, Texas, 1978.

Horowitz, Amy, and Lois W. Shindelman. *The Impact of Caring for an Elderly Relative*. New York, N.Y.: The Brookdale Center on Aging, Hunter College, 1980.

Horowitz, Amy, and Rose Dobrof. *The Role of Families in Providing Long Term Care to the Frail and Chronically Ill Elderly Living in the Community*. Final Report, grant from the Health Care Financing Administration, May 1982.

Johnson, Colleen Leahy, and Donald J. Catalano. "A Longitudinal Study of Family Supports to Impaired Elderly." *The Gerontologist*, vol. 23, 1983, pp. 612–618.

Kemper, Peter, et al. *Channeling Effects for an Early Sample at 6-Month Followup*. Princeton, N.J.: Mathematica Policy Research, Inc., May 1985 (revised).

———. *Research Design of the National Long Term Care Demonstration*. Princeton, N.J.: Mathematica Policy Research, Inc., November 1982.

Lewis, Mary Ann, Randee Bienenstock, Marjorie Cantor, and Elizabeth Schniewind. "The Extent to Which Informal and Formal Supports Interact to Maintain the Older People in the Community." Paper presented at the 33rd Annual Meeting of the Gerontological Society of America, November 24, 1980.

Monk, Abraham. "Family Supports in Old Age." *Social Work*, vol. 24, 1979, pp. 533–538.

Morris, John, Sylvia Sherwood, and Clarie Gutkin. *Meeting the Needs of the Impaired Elderly: The Power and Resiliency of the Informal Support System*. Final Report, grant from the Administration on Aging, November 1981.

Munnichs, Joep M. "Linkages of Old People with Their Families and Bureaucracy in a Welfare State, the Netherlands." In *Family Bureaucracy, and the Elderly*, ed. E. Shanas and M. Sussman, Durham, N.C.: Duke University Press, 1977.

National Center for Health Statistics. *Home Care for Persons 55 and Over*. Vital Health Statistics, series 10, no. 73, DHEW Publications no. (HSM) 72–1012, 1972.

Newman, Sandra, with James Morgan, Robert Marans, and Leon Pastalan. *Housing Adjustments of Older People: A Report of Findings from the Second Phase.* Ann Arbor, Mich.: Institute of Social Research, University of Michigan, 1976.

Paringer, Lynn. "The Forgotten Costs of Informal Long Term Care." Urban Institute Working Paper 1466-28, June 1983.

Poulshock, S. Walter. *The Effects on Families of Caring for Impaired Elderly in Residence.* Cleveland, Ohio: The Benjamin Rose Institute, 1982.

Poulshock, S. Walter, and Gary T. Deimling. "Families Caring for Elders in Residence: Issues in the Measurement of Burden." *Journal of Gerontology,* vol. 39, 1984, pp. 230–239.

Prager, Edward. "Subsidized Family Care of the Aged: U.S. Senate Bill 1161." *Policy Analysis,* vol. 4, 1978, pp. 477–490.

Public Opinion. "Opinion Roundup: Enduring Patterns in American Life: A Decade of NORC Surveys," vol. 5, no. 5, 1982, p. 25.

———. "Opinion Roundup: Personal Life Seems All Right," vol. 2, no. 1, 1979, p. 22.

Robinson, Betsy, and Majda Thurnher. "Taking Care of Aged Parents: A Family Cycle Transition." *The Gerontologist,* vol. 19, 1979, pp. 586–593.

Ruchlin, Hirsch S., John N. Morris, and Gerald M. Eggert. "Management and Financing of Long-Term Care Services: A New Approach to a Chronic Problem." *New England Journal of Medicine,* vol. 306, 1982, pp. 401–406.

Schorr, Alvin. " '. . . thy father and thy mother' A Second Look at Filial Responsibility and Family Policy." U.S. Department of Health and Human Services, Social Security Administration, Office of Policy, SSA Publication No. 13-11953, Washington, D.C.: July 1980.

Seelbach, Wayne C. "Gender Differences in Expectations for Filial Responsibility." *The Gerontologist,* vol. 17, 1977, pp. 421–425.

Shanas, Ethel. "The Family as a Social Support System in Old Age." *The Gerontologist,* vol. 19, 1979, pp. 169–174.

Soldo, Beth J., and Joana Myllyluoma. "Caregivers Who Live with Dependent Elderly." *The Gerontologist,* vol. 23, 1983, pp. 605–611.

Somers, Anne R. "Long-Term Care for the Elderly and Disabled: A New Health Priority." *New England Journal of Medicine,* vol. 307, 1982, pp. 221–226.

Stoller, Eleanor P., and Lorna L. Earl. "Help with Activities of Everyday Life: Sources of Support for Noninstitutionalized Elderly." *The Gerontologist,* vol. 23, 1983, pp. 64–70.

Sussman, Marvin B. "Incentives and Family Environment for the Elderly." Final Report to Administration on Aging, AOA Grant 90-A-316, Washington, D.C., February 1977.

Taber, Merlin A., Steve Anderson, and C. Jean Rogers. "Implementing Community Care in Illinois: Issues of Cost and Targeting in a Statewide Program." *The Gerontologist,* vol. 20, 1980, pp. 380–388.

Talbot, Maria, S. Amanda Smith, and Leonard Miller. "Informal Instrumental Support: Two Samples of California's Frail Low Income Elderly." Multipurpose Senior Services Project Evaluation, University of California, Berkeley, July 30, 1982.

Treas, Judith. "Family Support Systems for the Aged: Some Social and Demographic Considerations." *The Gerontologist,* vol. 17, 1977, pp. 486–491.

Urban Systems Research and Engineering, Inc. *In Home Services and the Contribution of Kin: Substitution Effects in Home Care Programs for the Elderly.* HHS-100-81-0026, May 1982.

U.S. Bureau of the Census. "America in Transition: An Aging Society." *Current Population Reports,* series P-23, no. 128. Washington, D.C.: U.S. Government Printing Office, 1983.

Wake, Sandra Byford, and Michael J. Sporakowski. "An Intergenerational Comparison of Attitudes Towards Supporting Aged Parents." *Journal of Marriage and the Family,* vol. 34, 1972, pp. 42–48.

Zarit, Steven H., Karen E. Reever, and Julie Bach-Peterson. "Relatives of the Impaired Elderly: Correlates of Feelings of Burden." *The Gerontologist,* vol. 20, 1980, pp. 649–655.

Index

Page numbers followed by *t* indicate tabular material; numbers followed by *n* indicate material in notes.

About the Authors

Jon B. Christianson is currently professor in the Department of Management and Public Policy and the Department of Economics at the University of Arizona. He is an economist and has concentrated on health-care policy issues. He has contributed to a number of journals, including *Health Services Research, New England Journal of Medicine, Medical Group Management,* and *Health Care Management Review,* and has authored or edited several monographs, including *Health Care Policy: A Political Economy Approach, Current Strategies for Containing Health Care Expenditures,* and *Competitive Contracting Processes in Indigent Medical Care Programs.* He has been involved with Mathematica Policy Research, Inc., in the evaluation design and analysis for the National Long-Term Care Demonstration since 1980, with primary responsibility for the analysis of program implementation and its impacts on informal caregiving and caregiver well-being. He received his bachelor's degree in mathematics and economics from St. Olaf College and his master's degree and doctorate in economics from the University of Wisconsin. Prior to joining the faculty at the University of Arizona, he was associate professor in the Department of Agricultural Economics and Economics at Montana State University.

Susan A. Stephens is currently a senior survey researcher at Mathematica Policy Research, Inc., and has been involved in the survey design for the National Long-Term Care Demonstration evaluation, particularly for the surveys of both the elderly participants and their informal caregivers. She is a sociologist with a concentration in survey methodology, and has also conducted research in the areas of urban development, neighborhood revitalization, and programs for disabled persons. She received her bachelor's degree in sociology and psychology from Reed College and her master's degree and doctorate in sociology from the University of Michigan. Prior to joining Mathematica, she was assistant professor of sociology and director of the Indianapolis Area Project at Indiana University in Bloomington, Indiana.